MEGATUDES

BILLY RIGGS

MEGATUDES

—TWELVE—
CRITICAL ATTITUDES THAT
WILL SHAPE YOUR FUTURE

Megatudes
Twelve Critical Attitudes That Will Shape Your Future

Published by:
Tremendous Life Books
118 West Allen Street
Mechanicsburg, PA 17055

717-766-9499   800-233-2665
Fax: 717-766-6565

www.TremendousLifeBooks.com

ISBN: 978-1-936354-36-8

TABLE OF CONTENTS

INTRODUCTION. 7

Chapter I
THE WELL OF THE MIND 11

Chapter II
AN ATTITUDE OF VISION 31

Chapter III
AN ATTITUDE OF STEADY PROGRESS. 49

Chapter IV
AN ATTITUDE OF INTEGRITY. 65

Chapter V
AN ATTITUDE OF INTIMACY 77

Chapter VI
AN ATTITUDE OF PROACTIVITY. 87

Chapter VII
AN ATTITUDE OF POSITIVITY 101

Chapter VIII
AN ATTITUDE OF AUTHENTICITY 117

Chapter IX
AN ATTITUDE OF RESPONSIBILITY 133

Chapter X
AN ATTITUDE OF OPTIMISM 143

Chapter XI
AN ATTITUDE OF CONFIDENCE. 159

Chapter XII
AN ATTITUDE OF PURPOSE 175

Chapter XIII
AN ATTITUDE OF PERSISTENCE 191

INTRODUCTION

Attitude is everything. Attitude lies at the core of a happy and productive life. There is no situation so dreadful that a proper attitude will not soften the blow. There is no circumstance so pleasant that a bad one cannot rob it of its luster, or even spoil it. In my thirties, I decided to become a recreational pilot. Just for the fun of it, I took lessons and began flying a small Cessna 152 out of and around my hometown of Raleigh, North Carolina. As I learned to fly, my instructor properly indoctrinated me with the skills, knowledge and terminology necessary to safely command an aircraft. Of particular interest to me was an aviator's peculiar use of the word "attitude." To a pilot, the term has a very narrow meaning, and it has nothing to do with his or her disposition. Attitude, to a flier, refers to the plane's angle of attack, the trajectory at which an aircraft approaches the horizon, and there are only three possible attitudes an airplane can have:

1) Nose up—which usually means the aircraft is climbing,

2) Straight and level—neither climbing nor descending, and

3) Nose down—which is the normal configuration for descent.

In aviation, therefore, it's not just a cliché; your attitude *really does* determine (or at least heavily influence) your altitude. Similarly, outside the cockpit, it is the manner in which you approach your circumstances, rather than the nature of the circumstances themselves that dictates the heights to which you might climb or the depths to which you will fall. It is your attitude, your angle of attack, your interpretation and vantage point that makes all the difference. Only a small percentage of life is about what happens to you. It is overwhelmingly about how you *view, approach and respond to* what happens to you.

There are about a dozen attitudes that are critical to a balanced, happy, and productive life. They are so important that I call them *Megatudes*. A person who embodies them all has chosen a trajectory that will ultimately bring him the fulfillment for which all human beings yearn. Exhibit only a few of them and you will miss out on much of the joy you might otherwise have known. Reject them all, and you have doomed yourself to a bitter, lonely, and empty existence, and have set your one-and-only life on a course for misery. Whatever your current path may be, you have chosen it for yourself in the attitudes you embrace. The road to change begins with a transformation of your *attitude*. But it is a toll road, and admission is gained only by your earnest decision to infuse your heart, mind, and behavior with life's Megatudes.

Chapter I

THE WELL
OF THE MIND

Happiness and success, the crown jewels of life, are universally sought for ourselves and envied in others. But these twin gems are not bestowed by fate or luck. Nor are they often the result of happenstance. They are not even a divine gift. Rather, they are drawn from the well of each person's *own mind*. The attitudes stored there comprise the source from which all of life streams. Thus, if your well is poisoned, the water removed from it will be bitter to you and toxic to others. But if the well is untainted, everything that flows from it will be pure, refreshing, and restorative. This is the fundamental principle of life. If you miss this, then you will miss out on most of the wonderful things life has to offer.

In my youth I heard an old Baptist preacher named Vance Havner voice one of his favorite sayings: "What's down in the well comes up in the bucket." Stated another way, whatever is deep inside your mind will eventually find expression in your words and deeds which will, over the years, create a life that is gradually becoming more desirable or depressing. A pessimistic view of life lodged in the recesses of your mind exerts a relentless gravitational pull on your career, your relationships, and your spirit. Like a millstone around your neck, it makes every task harder and prevents you from realizing your potential in life. A victim mentality hidden in the crevices of your brain inevitably oozes out through your hands, feet, and mouth, affects your choices, and paralyzes your potential. The effect of this negativity functions much like the HIV virus. It is not the infection itself that kills you, but the weakening effect it has on your entire system, leaving you vulnerable to setbacks that otherwise might not be considered serious, let alone fatal. Those with a polluted well have thus rendered themselves helpless in the face of minor setbacks, obstacles, and challenges. Decade after decade, the many thousands of poor decisions made in response to misguided attitudes accumulate like so many snowflakes into monstrous drifts of sorrow and regret. But a positive outlook on life and a wholesale acceptance of personal responsibility for your actions *and their consequences* will similarly produce behaviors that predictably result in success and happiness. The proper maintenance of your well holds the key to fulfillment.

The preacher's axiom was true, but so is its unavoidable corollary: "Whatever comes up in the bucket reveals what is down in your well." If you wish to know the contents of your subconscious mind, you need look no further than your own behavior. Your actions are a strong indicator of the contents of your mind. Before continuing your reading of this book, it is essential that you take a long look in your "bucket."

Examine your life. Are you happy? Are your relationships deep and meaningful? Are you successful? If your answer to any of these questions is "no" or a qualified "yes," then you are missing at least one of life's twelve "Megatudes," the all-important attitudes that shape destinies. You must resist the temptation to blame others for your plight. Refuse to give in to the notion that success is unattainable due to circumstances beyond your control or that happiness is out of your reach because fate dealt you a lousy hand. Just *look* in your bucket. What you see reflected back to you in the water's surface will almost perfectly match the contents of your well, your mind. The problem rests there and perhaps nowhere else.

For this reason, the key to improving your life situation lies within the confines of your own skull. The polluted waters that seep relentlessly into your relationships must be purified. The steady drip, drip, drip of negativity that erodes your motivation must be shut off at the source. The muddy waters that cloud your judgment and color your view of the world must be cleansed. The nagging voices (from within and without) that dam up your potential must be silenced or ignored. Once the source is decontaminated, the new, pure flow will slowly fill your spirit and then overflow into the world around you. The mighty oak tree of your dreams must be fed from the waters of your well; the purer the water, the more majestic the tree.

The groundbreaking American psychologist and philosopher, William James, once said: "The greatest discovery of my generation is that human beings can alter their lives by altering their attitudes of mind." Amazingly, Dr. James said that *more than one hundred years ago!* Therefore, the greatest failure of this current generation is that more than a century after this earth-shattering discovery was made most people still haven't accepted the reality of it. By comparison, the automobile is about 115 years old, and it was in widespread use in a matter of decades. The airplane was invented in 1903, and now everyone takes air travel for granted. About that same time, the existence of the germ was demonstrated to be the cause of contagious diseases; no one doubts this. The computer is only a few decades old, yet almost everyone uses one. The Internet and cellular phones were only invented recently, and today we can't live without them. iPads didn't exist a decade ago, yet now we are surrounded by them. Why, then, have we proven to be so resistant to the fact that attitude profoundly affects life? Ironically, it is because the human "well" is contaminated with a bias to believe that attitude matters little.

The psychologically healthy person ruthlessly disciplines himself to cling to the belief that "your attitude determines your altitude." Without such determination, this essential belief will slip from your grasp, because it is the natural state of the human mind to blame all of life's ills on circumstances that are beyond our control. In this way, a self-defeating belief system is born in which outside circumstances drag us into failure, and then provide an all-too convenient excuse for laziness and failure. Those who fail often do so because they believed success was impossible due to outside factors. This victim mentality robs us of our motivation, for why bother to play the game if the deck is stacked against us and the outcome is already determined? The result of this poisonous belief system is *inaction*, which not only causes failure but, in turn, becomes the excuse for further inaction. Like an airplane without power, the man with the poisoned well begins a slow downward death spiral with a predictable and painful result.

It is far easier to fail and then blame outside factors than it is to discipline ourselves to work hard, taking full responsibility for our actions (even actions taken by other people that affect us) and their consequences. But the mental strain of cleaning and maintaining our mental well, while more difficult in the short term, pays huge dividends in the distant future. It produces a better you and brighter fortunes. Therefore, a choice is to be made and it is one of cosmic proportions for you and for your future. It is *not* a choice between pain and ease, for the human experience provides no options that are free from pain. The question is never whether to endure pain or avoid it. Rather, it is the choice between the short-term pain of self-control and the long-term one of disappointment. Which pain will you choose to endure, the self-inflicted discomfort of discipline (which tends to decrease over time), or the ever-growing sting of regret?

Discipline and discomfort are inextricably bundled together. Discipline means getting out of bed when you'd rather sleep in, working when you'd rather watch TV, exercising when you want to catch a movie, drinking coffee and pressing on when you're tempted to take a nap, eating fruit when you crave doughnuts. All of these bring discomfort. But it is the *lack* of discipline that causes the greater distress, for the man who chooses the easier path in the short term has sentenced himself to even greater pain in the long one. The woman who chose to sleep late, eat fatty foods, and take it easy will spend her entire life playing "would-a, could-a, should-a." The individual who cannot or will not master himself is doomed to mediocrity or worse. He or she will live out the "golden years" thinking "if only I had worked harder," "if only I had quit smoking sooner," "if only I had pursued my goals more vigorously," "if only I had acted on that idea when I had it." As John Greenleaf Whittier wrote: "For all sad words of tongue and pen, the saddest are these: 'it might have been.'" The bad things we have done can be forgiven, and regrets for them can usually be forgotten and left in the past. But the regret for those opportunities passed up, those dreams not pursued, those chances not taken lingers and festers over the passing years as the consequences of inaction become more and more apparent, and the gap between what we are and what we could have been widens.

Your ability to take the crucial step of disciplining yourself consistently is profoundly affected—if not completely determined—by your state of mind. If the waters of pessimism flow freely from your well, you will be unable to motivate yourself to take the difficult steps necessary to succeed. When your alarm clock sounds before dawn, signaling your need to bound from bed and pursue your dreams, the voice of cynicism will echo from the depths of the well to dampen your enthusiasm: "What's the use? Why should I get up early and try my hardest? It's not going to make any difference anyway. I might as well just stay right here in bed. If I'm going to be a failure, I might as well be a warm, well-rested one. Better to be a relaxed loser than a stressed-out one." When the plate of cupcakes is passed before you, your willpower to resist temptation will be weakened by the voice from your well: "I've been overweight for years. That's never going to change. I know I'll just gain a little weight every year for the rest of my life, so why torture myself? If I'm going to be fat anyway, I'm darn well going to enjoy myself getting there!" If, on the other hand, the voice from the well is an encouraging one, your willpower will be strengthened: "The future is bright, and it is largely under my control. The quality of life I live will be determined by the decisions I make and the actions I take. I can do anything I set my mind to. What I do today will positively impact my life and bring me closer to fulfilling my goals and dreams." The key to drawing success and happiness from your "bucket" lies in your ability to transform the contents of your well.

It is one of life's most formidable challenges that the water in your well, left untended, gradually becomes dirtier, not cleaner. The Second Law of Thermodynamics works as unfailingly on the human mind as it does on the physical world: everything tends to move from a state of order to one of disorder. A home that is not routinely cleaned and straightened will slowly, inexorably become messier. Even though you may toil until your home is spotless, the moment you stop cleaning the process toward disarray immediately begins again. The longer you wait between house cleanings, the greater the task will become. A body that is not regularly bathed will gradually attract dirt, germs and odors. But a thorough shower does not stop the progression; it merely interrupts it and sets it back a few hours. The moment you step out of the tub it begins anew. Just as your home and your body must be routinely cleaned, the water in your well must be continually filtered and purified.

The task of correctly maintaining your well is similar to that of the proper care of a swimming pool. If a pool owner does not monitor the quality of the water and maintain it on a regular basis, it will become murky and the sides of the pool will feel slimy. Leaves will float on the surface or cover the bottom. The pH balance will become too high or too low, which causes swimmers' skin to itch or the pumps to deteriorate. The filter will become clogged with debris and the water will emit a faint odor. If the owner were to leave the country for a year, on his return the pool would be filled with algae, dirt, and bacteria. The clean-up job would be enormous. Similarly, the contents of your mental well, if left unchecked, will not remain static. They will slide relentlessly into negativity, pessimism, and cynicism. Unless you take specific steps to avoid this, the compounded effect of years of neglecting your well will be failure, bitterness, and resignation. Just as you set aside time to bathe your body and tidy your home you must regularly schedule activities that *cleanse your thoughts*. But first, you need to analyze the contents of the well, itself.

The proper analysis of your well water comes easily: you need merely to monitor your self-talk, the words that you whisper under your breath or say silently in your mind about yourself and the world. *"I'm so stupid." "Why can't I do anything right?" "I am such a loser!" "Nobody wants to be my friend." "Why should I bother working harder? It won't change anything."* More often, the message is not even put into words; it is merely a feeling, whether of dread, helplessness, or under-confidence. What messages are you hearing or feeling? What does your inner voice say? Is the message positive or negative? Is it helpful or unhelpful? Chances are, unless you have been deliberately planting good thoughts in your subconscious mind, the messages are overwhelmingly negative. Most people spend a lifetime bombarding themselves with self-defeating messages. No one taught them to be negative or pessimistic; that comes naturally, making it quite challenging for the average person to remain upbeat and confident. It is hard work—though profoundly rewarding—to transform yourself into a person who is positive and upbeat. Just as an untended garden is inevitably invaded and overtaken by weeds, your unguarded mind will unavoidably be overrun by negativity. Only strenuous, regular, relentless hoeing, weeding, and planting will produce the harvest you desire. There is a transition that must be made. You must progress from "Negatudes," through and beyond "Metatudes," and arrive at the pinnacle of healthy mental living: *Megatudes.*

THE NEGATUDE: I CAN'T

Not all self-talk is necessarily damaging. There are at least four types of self-talk statements:

1) I can't,

2) I shouldn't,

3) I won't, and

4) I am.

The first two are harmful and the remaining two are beneficial. The most destructive kind of self-talk is the "I can't" or "I don't" statement. "I can't succeed." "I can't make enough money to pay these bills." "I can't lose weight." "I don't have what it takes." "I don't have the talent for that." "I don't have the motivation to achieve my dreams." Regrettably, not only are these the most damaging statements you can utter to yourself, they are also the most common. They flow effortlessly into and through our minds, strewing the debris of doubt throughout the psyche and undermining confidence. Unless their flow is reduced or redirected, they will cut well-worn ruts in your brain, and with each passing year the ruts will widen and deepen to channel even more potent currents, all emptying into the same stagnant pool of hopelessness.

There are two other types of self-talk that represent a reduction in self-inflicted harm, but still fall short of the ideal. Call them Metatudes if you like, intermediate stages in the metamorphosis of your well. Consider them transitional links in the evolutionary chain that leads to and culminates in full-blown self-actualization. Stopping at one of these waypoints will maroon you in an existence that falls short of the ultimate fulfillment you seek. Metaphorically, these next two "halfway houses" are tantamount to crawling on your belly like a lizard or walking on your hind feet and knuckles like an ape rather than standing erect and striding on two feet as a human being can and should. The first middle-of-the-road stage is the weaker of the two.

METATUDE I: I SHOULDN'T

Still damaging, but less obviously so than the "I can't" message, is the "I shouldn't" or "I should" statement. *"I shouldn't eat this." "I should exercise today." "I should get up early and get a head start on my work." "I really shouldn't go out tonight; I have an early class tomorrow." "I should do my homework first."* On the surface, these statements seem like a positive step. In reality, they merely conceal the unspoken end of the sentence, the part that starts with "but." For example, a woman who has been dieting for three weeks is invited by a friend to join her friends at a Mexican Restaurant. She replies, "I really shouldn't do this…." The friend instantly knows that the answer is yes, just a reluctant, guilt-ridden acquiescence instead of an enthusiastic endorsement of the plan. "I shouldn't eat this," if the thought were fully completed, would read, "I shouldn't eat this, but I'm going to anyway." The self-talk is still one of resignation to failure. Much stronger is the "I won't" statement.

METATUDE II: I WON'T

I won't (or I will) statements represent a volitional commitment to follow a particular path. This type of inner declaration leaves no doubt; there are no hidden meanings, concealed predicates, or unspoken escape clauses. There is no wiggle room in the "I won't" statement. When the invitation to violate the terms of the diet arises, the woman no longer replies, "I shouldn't (implying she probably will, anyway)...." Instead she responds, "Thank you for the invitation, but I won't put myself in that situation." The high school student states, "I will do my homework first, then go play basketball afterwards." The reformed sloth emphatically says to himself, "I will exercise today at 10:00 a.m., *period*." The college freshman vows silently to herself, "I will be in bed by 11:00 p.m. so I'll feel rested for my test tomorrow morning." The most powerful statement of all, however, is the "I am" statement.

THE MEGATUDE: I AM

When you choose the "I am" statement, you have moved beyond the realm of simply controlling your behavior to establishing and reinforcing your identity. Notice the spectrum of self-talk proclamations as they progress from victimization to reluctant surrender to determination to character.

Negatude	Victimization	*"I can't stop eating sweets."*
Metatude I	Reluctant Surrender	*"I shouldn't keep eating sweets."*
Metatude II	Determination	*"I won't eat any sweets today."*
MEGATUDE	Character	*"I am a healthy eater."*

Once I begin to see myself, by very nature, as a healthy eater rather than someone with the mere willpower to

21

deny myself the pleasure of dessert now and then, saying no becomes your normal response. I am no longer one who drags his body to the gym and forces himself to exercise; to the contrary, I am a body-builder! I am not one who resists the temptation to smoke; I am a non-smoker. I am not simply one who disciplines himself to study; I am a model student. Once you make it a habit to use *I am* statements, you begin to shape your self-image, and self-image is destiny. However, if you are—like most people—in the habit of using self-defeating statements, there are three steps necessary for the purification of your well.

1) GUARD AGAINST BAD INPUT

A swimming pool, in the off-season, is sometimes covered to prevent trash from blowing into it. Each autumn, leaves fall on that cover. Swirling winds sometimes blow dust and litter on it. It is impossible to prevent the rubbish of the world from coming in contact with the pool, but that is not a major concern when the cover is there to do its job. Waste that brushes across the cover is not to be feared. It is only that which enters the water that causes problems. It is similarly impossible to keep negative influences from swirling around us, or to prevent the acid rain of criticism from occasionally catching us in a downpour. But as the keeper of your well, it is imperative that you prevent such input from going any farther than skin deep. As the saying goes, "You can't stop birds from flying overhead, but you *can* keep them from building a nest in your hair."

Negativity will seep into your soul unless it is rejected outright. The human brain behaves like a dry sponge when it is exposed to pessimism and hopelessness, eagerly soaking it up. Uplifting, encouraging messages, however, tend to be less readily absorbed. It might take months or years for the brain to internalize a positive thought and accept it as reality. This natural receptivity to harmful thoughts and resistance to helpful ones demands that you constantly remain vigilant about controlling what goes into your brain. Like milk, which descends gradually but steadily toward spoilage the moment it is opened, your brain will tend toward doom and gloom unless you diligently protect it from life's souring influences. Because negative thoughts are much more quickly absorbed than positive ones, great care must be taken to keep the negative thoughts away from your "sponge" long enough for the positive ones to lodge there. But how is this accomplished?

When discouraging words are spoken by others or wander unsolicited through your mind, you must respond with an instant and non-negotiable rebuttal, moving quickly to positive thoughts and solutions. In what amounts to a game of mental "hot potato," the *moment* you recognize a thought as being cynical or pessimistic or harmful, you must instantly reject it. If you dwell on these thoughts, your subconscious mind will welcome them and internalize them; they will set like concrete and transform themselves from mere passing thoughts into an intransigent world view. You will gradually begin to see all of existence through the lens of negativism, hopelessness, and helplessness, and your behavior will reflect this. But if you stubbornly refuse to listen to the discouraging voices, the positive ones will slowly replace them.

2) PURIFY THE CONTENTS OF YOUR WELL

The filters in a swimming pool continually cycle the water to remove contaminants that managed to get into it despite the presence of the cover. When the filter is running, impure water is removed and slowly replaced by clean. Similarly, your mind has, over the years, accumulated the debris of destructive beliefs and the scum of low expectations. But the filters you'll need to extract these negative influences from your brain do not function automatically. Rather, they must be set in motion as an act of your will and imposed on your mind continually. The unhelpful beliefs you harbor in your mind must be slowly eroded by the strong, steady flow of positive thoughts through your consciousness. Like a cult member who must be deprogrammed via many hours of being hammered by truth, you must flood your brain with uplifting and positive messages.

In order to reprogram your subconscious mind, you must discipline yourself to immediately replace every disheartening statement delivered by your self-talk with an accurate statement. Though most of the self-defeating messages housed in your psyche are gross exaggerations, each time they are whispered unchallenged by your subconscious mind the message they carry is reinforced. So powerful are these messages that it generally takes about *five positive messages* to overcome just one negative one. If other people are not providing these positive counterbalances, we must work daily to provide them for ourselves. The result is predictable: negative statements become slightly truer of you each time, because they drag down your performance. Just as a man who believes he is ugly actually *becomes* less confident and outgoing, making him less attractive to potential girlfriends, a person who genuinely believes he is a loser will eventually, slowly, almost inevitably become one. This is why it is vital that you challenge these messages vigorously.

Each self-destructive statement must be challenged the moment it emerges from your well. It must be forcefully replaced with an accurate statement. If your inner pessimist says, "I'm so boring that no one would ever want to be my friend," you must instantly replace that statement with a more accurate one: "I'm probably not the most interesting person in town, but people far less interesting than me have many loving friends." When the voice tells you, "I'm just not smart enough to succeed," substitute the truth: "I'm no Einstein, but plenty of people who are no smarter than I am are succeeding greatly. I just have to apply myself and persevere and I'll probably succeed, too." If you hear your inner voice saying, "I'm so ugly no one will ever want to marry me," respond instantly with this: "Lots of people who are far less attractive than me are married, so I'm actually quite a catch." This exercise must be performed repeatedly, day after day, until the positive messages overwhelm the detrimental ones.

The words you choose to use to describe your circumstances are important, too. When you refer to a difficult situation in a negative manner, calling it a "problem," the result is discouragement and frustration. However, if you force yourself to refer to the very same situation as a "challenge," your central nervous system instantly responds by pumping adrenaline into your bloodstream, summoning your resources, and mustering your courage. Labeling a circumstance as an obstacle is counterproductive; seeing it as a hurdle to be surmounted is exhilarating! Terms like unfair, unjust, breakdown, trouble, failure, setback, predicament, headache, aggravation, and hindrance can similarly drain you of resolve. These must be banished from your internal vocabulary and replaced with their more uplifting equivalents: a call to arms, a dare, an opportunity to prove your mettle, a gut check, a tryout, a contest, the chance to prove yourself, a test of your abilities, the opportunity to *really* earn your paycheck. An adversary has not "threatened" you; he has thrown down the gauntlet. You have been called out, and you must respond with your very best effort. The key to your ultimate success is changing your thinking from negative to positive in every aspect of your life.

3) PROTECT AGAINST FUTURE CONTAMINATION

Finally, in order to keep a pool clear and sparkling and prohibit the growth of bacteria, pool owners add special chemicals to the water from time to time. In the same way, to prevent the regeneration of toxins in your well, you must continually pour helpful content into it. This requires a systematic plan that must be adhered to throughout life. Just as the chemicals must be added every several days for as long as a pool exists, discouragement must be flushed from your well on a consistent basis for as long as you live. If you want to experience a happy and successful life, you must accept this as reality. These are unavoidable realities of human life: you must breathe every few seconds, you must eat every few hours, you must sleep every night and you must *force positive messages into your brain every few days*. There are four means of doing so.

First, you should have a list of motivational books that you plan to read or listen to. Of course, there are the classics that have inspired millions over many decades. Among these are Earl Nightingale's *The Strangest Secret*. Others are:

As a Man Thinketh
by James Allen

The Magic of Believing
by Claude Bristol

How to Win Friends and Influence People
by Dale Carnegie

Acres of Diamonds
by Russell Conwell

The Richest Man in Babylon
by George S. Clason

Think and Grow Rich
by Napoleon Hill

The Greatest Salesman in the World
by Og Mandino

The Power of Positive Thinking
by Norman Vincent Peale

The Magic of Thinking Big
by David J. Schwartz

The Psychology of Winning
by Dennis Waitley

See You at the Top
by Zig Ziglar

Believe and Achieve
by W. Clement Stone

I recommend that you buy them all and read them regularly, over and over, until their message becomes your own. If you can't afford to buy them, check them out of your public library. Some of these classics are available in an audio format for purchase or download. You should also supplement these classics with other motivational books (like this one) to get a more modern treatment of the subject. Financial guru Dave Ramsey estimates that the average millionaire reads about one non-fiction book each month. It is no coincidence that the rich and successful are almost obsessive about personal development.

Secondly, you should listen regularly to motivational messages. There are literally hundreds (probably thousands) of inspirational speakers who have each produced audio messages that can be purchased in bookstores or over the web. A simple Internet search will yield a banner harvest of such messages for download or on compact discs that will transform your commute to and from work into a master's degree course in success. According to motivational speaker Zig Ziglar, if you want to fully absorb the content of an audio message, you must listen to it at least 17 times. As these encouraging words pour forth daily from your car speakers, they will relentlessly attack the negative ones that have made your brain their home for many years.

Thirdly, make it your habit to attend motivational conferences whenever you can squeeze it into your schedule. There are well-known seminars that annually appear in auditoriums in cities all over the U.S. featuring the premiere motivators of our time. Even if you've heard the speakers before, simply bathing yourself for an entire day in positive input has the effect of reprogramming your brain. Each time you hear the messages, you will draw new insights and emphases from them. Motivation is like a meal—it doesn't last very long but is, nonetheless, absolutely essential. You must feed your need for inspiration as regularly as you feed your body's requirement for nourishment. Each time you fill your well with uplifting input, you refresh the water there, improving the quality of life that you draw from it.

Finally, organize your schedule to stay in constant contact with those people in your life who naturally encourage and motivate you. Regrettably, there are those who routinely poison the wells of their friends, relatives, and coworkers with doubts and fears. You must limit your exposure to the toxic waste that is so readily available in the bad attitudes of others. Identify those who drain your energy and sap your motivation, and think of creative ways to shield yourself from their influence. Think of those whose positive demeanor brings a smile to your face and fans the flames of confidence and determination within you. It is people like these who will act as "chlorine for the brain," overwhelming your fears and doubts with self-assurance, purpose, and resolve.

There are at least twelve specific Megatudes—supremely important attitudes—that will emerge from a properly maintained well, slowly turning your desert-like existence into a fertile and flourishing garden. By studying each of the next twelve chapters you will learn how to recognize these traits in your own life, or note their absence. When you discover one that is missing, you will then be able to identify the types of input that you must avoid or actively seek out to replace the misguided thinking that holds you back. It is a long and arduous task to replace the damaging thought processes infecting your brain, but it is a necessary one for anyone who hopes to live a truly fulfilled life.

EXERCISE: Every morning, say the following words to yourself:

Today is a very important day, because what I do today will change my future. The choices I make today—even the small ones—will either make my life better or they will make it worse, so I will choose wisely. The decisions I make today will either advance *my career or damage it; they will improve my relationships or harm them; they will increase my income or decrease it; they will improve my health or undermine it; they will enhance my reputation or soil it; they will strengthen my character or weaken it; they will either sweeten my well or they will contaminate it. Therefore, I will carefully consider how I spend my time today, what I say, how I say it, what I do, with whom I spend my time and what I put in my body. I will plan my day according to my priorities, rather than let it be planned for me by pressures or by the demands of others. I will guard my mind from negativity and pessimism, because whatever I allow to pollute my well will eventually pollute my life. I will flood my mind with positive thoughts and input. I will expect good things to happen. I will face each challenge with calmness, clarity, and a smile. Today is, indeed, a VERY important day.**

*For your convenience, this page is repeated at the end of this book so that you can cut it out and post it where you will see it every day.

Chapter II

An Attitude
of Vision

Life is like a bicycle; it derives its stability from forward motion. What is true of your life as a whole is also true of your career or business. Like a spinning top that wobbles as it slows, a person who takes too much time to relax and rest will eventually feel life becoming more and more unstable. Year by year, almost imperceptibly, progress will come to a grinding halt. For this reason, it is essential that you accept the unchanging reality that you are either actively building a better life or, through your inactivity, life is slowly getting worse. In this regard, the law of inertia exerts its influence on your life just as it does the physical world: an object (or person) at rest tends to remain at rest, and an object in motion tends to remain in motion, unless acted upon by an outside force. This is why the struggles of unsuccessful people tend to multiply. The slower their progress becomes, the more likely it becomes that they will slow even further, and the harder it becomes to reverse the trend. Success and failure, alike, tend to accelerate exponentially. This is also why successful people usually move from one success to the next. They enjoy the luxury of being propelled into the future, surfing on the wave of forward momentum that their past actions have created. The momentum earned through past efforts has purchased for them the privilege of "coasting" from time to time in the present and even more in the future.

However, this momentum cannot be created—much less sustained—without proper motivation. For some, the driving force that propels them comes from living life paycheck-to-paycheck, fearing bankruptcy or homelessness. For others, the catalyst for action is a demanding boss and the acute awareness that a pink slip might be their reward for even the slightest slip-up. Still others, like those in social work, ministry, or education, the inspiration for tireless work is the betterment of society, the good of other people, or the belief that they are pleasing God. But your motivation will only reach its zenith when its source is a personal vision that is of vital importance *to you*. This is where the inertia illustration in the previous paragraph fails: in the physical world, inertia may only be overcome by an outside force. In the human sphere, it is overcome best by an *inside* force. Negative inertia relinquishes its stranglehold on your growth in response to an unrelenting determination in your soul. It succumbs to a positive vision of life, a soul-encompassing dream, a magnificent obsession. Such a vision can emerge from only one place: your well.

Inferior motives often beget unfulfilled lives. The woman who works late into the night and then brings work home for the evening in order to please an austere boss is probably driven by fear—fear that she is not worthy of a better job and lucky to have the one she does. On the giant silver screen of her imagination she sees herself scanning the want ads every morning, pounding the pavement week after week, searching in vain for even a menial job to pay her bills. The tape loop in her brain depicts her being rejected again and again by interviewers who shake their heads sadly, telling her she just doesn't have what it takes. Her mental movie's predictable climax is reached when she runs completely out of money and becomes destitute. This is her vision of life. It motivates her to work diligently where she is, frantically running in place, but seldom moving forward. The man who slaves day after day, just barely getting by, is also motivated by fear. The driving vision he sees in his mind is one of embarrassment, failure, and loss. Each day on the 60-inch plasma screen of his psyche he sees eviction from his home, the repossession of his car, the loss of what few possessions he has, the collapse of his family. He imagines the neighbors shaking their heads in pity, and his family members whispering to one another about what a loser he is. Whatever he usually envisions about his future is, by definition, his life *vision*. This fearful image is the impetus for his survival, but not for success. Similarly, whatever *you* regularly envision about your future automatically becomes *your* vision.

In each of these two scenarios, the waters flowing from the well have been clouded by self-doubt, and the impure contents of the well have manifested themselves as mediocrity or failure. Your vision of life, hidden in your mind whether you are consciously aware of it or not, is not merely a way of looking at things, it is your *destiny*, because it almost always grows into a self-fulfilling prophecy. What's down in the well, and *only* what's down in the well, can possibly come up in the bucket. It is impossible to draw clear water from a murky well. Likewise, it is ludicrous to see the filthy water of failure that has "come up in the bucket" (that is, become your current life situation), but nevertheless declare that your well is pure and untainted.

Highly-successful people are invariably driven by a dream, a goal that is of profound importance to them. But vision alone deteriorates into mere daydreaming unless it is coupled with diligent work. Mere vision transforms into a life-shaping Megatude only when it burns so deeply in the soul that it propels, for example, a musician to practice the guitar until his fingers bleed, or an athlete to lift weights to the point of utter exhaustion, or a business owner to toil late into the night and live on little sleep for years on end. This level of motivation causes a few otherwise ordinary people to rise above those with superior gifts, intelligence, or opportunities. Almost all of the world's best musicians, athletes, poets, actors, chess players, and writers, driven by a vision to be the best, slogged away endless hours in obscurity. Known as the "10,000-Hour Rule," this principle observes that the world's elite in every area of endeavor practiced their craft at least 10,000 hours in order to reach the top. As Eddie Cantor, the singing star of early radio and Broadway, said, "It takes twenty years to make an overnight success." The list of examples is impressive.

> **Ray Bradbury,** the acclaimed author of *Fahrenheit 451* and scores of other science fiction books and short stories, began writing 1,000 words every day at the age of 12 and continued into old age.

> **Jerry Rice,** the greatest receiver in the history of the National Football League, was passed over by 20

teams because he was deemed too slow and too small to compete. But his practice regimen was so intense that those who tried to keep up with him often became sick from exhaustion.

Wayne Gretzky, known to hockey fans as "The Great One," was renowned for his habit of being the first one to arrive at practice each day and the last one to leave, even after being recognized as the best hockey player of all time.

Tiger Woods, arguably the greatest golfer of our generation, works out or practices golf from 6:30 a.m. until 7:00 p.m. every day.

Bill Gates learned in the 11th grade that there was a computer terminal at the University of Washington that sat unused from 2:00 a.m. until 6:00 a.m. every day. Since computers were few and far between in those days, he seized the opportunity to hone his skills. He regularly set his alarm clock for 1:30 a.m., when he secretly slipped out the window of his bedroom, walked two miles to the university and practiced programming until 6:00 a.m. He would then sneak back home and crawl into his bed, only to be awakened by his mother a few minutes later for school.

The Beatles performed for five and a half hours every night, seven nights a week, for 27 straight months at four clubs in Hamburg, Germany before becoming famous. This amounts to 1,200 concerts before they ever came to America. By comparison, The Rolling Stones have played only about twice that many concerts *in 50 years!*

Bobby Fisher was a chess grandmaster by the age of 16, but by that time he had already been studying relentlessly for 9 years.

Michael Phelps, who won eight gold medals in the Beijing Olympics in 2008, swims for six hours a day, six days a week, without fail.

Pablo Casals, the greatest cellist who ever lived, practiced six hours a day even at the age of 95.

Thomas Edison's typical work day lasted 18 hours. It is no wonder that he was issued 1,093 patents.

Liu Shikun, one of China's most brilliant pianists, was imprisoned from 1949 until 1956 for his refusal to renounce western music. Though denied a piano for those seven years, he nonetheless emerged as an even better pianist than before. How? He spent those seven years practicing relentlessly every piano piece he had ever learned—on an imaginary piano!

Winston Churchill, one of the 20th century's greatest orators, was known to practice his speeches almost obsessively.

Jeffrey Immelt, CEO of General Electric, has maintained a work schedule averaging 100 hours per week for more than 25 years.

Warren Buffet, one of the world's greatest investors, is renowned for his daily routine that includes hours poring over graphs, charts, and articles looking for investment opportunities.

Every great leader or highly successful person is marked by a clear vision and an unending zeal to make it come true.

Such an obsession drove Alexander the Great to conquer the world by age 33, and Abraham Lincoln to persevere through the Civil War to preserve the Union. Mother Teresa was motivated by spiritual passion to give up all her worldly belongings and move to the ghetto of Calcutta, India, where she spent decades ministering to the poor, the orphaned, and the dying. Billy Graham invested a lifetime of effort in his quest to promote the gospel. At the opposite end of this spectrum lies Adolph Hitler, whose sick and twisted passion was to rid the world of the Jewish people and establish Germany as the dominant power in Europe. Those who impact the world, whether for good or for ill, do so not so much because of their personality, intelligence, looks, or talent, but because of the intensity of their drive and motivation.

Leaders who are driven by grand visions succeed in direct proportion to their ability to infect the people around them with their dream. A classic example of this phenomenon was Martin Luther King, Jr., who stood on the steps of the Lincoln Memorial in Washington, DC and declared, "I have a dream, that this nation under God shall rise up and live out the true meaning of her creed: We hold these truths to be self-evident, that all men are created equal...." Such dreams are contagious because they are noble, rather than self-centered ones. People are magnetically drawn to those who passionately hold dreams that are great and good, believing that those who catch such visions are made better by them. Even Hitler expressed his dream of a powerful and prosperous Germany in beautiful and glowing terms, conveniently failing to mention his murderous intentions. So soaring was his rhetoric and so inspired were the masses by his vision that he was elected Chancellor of Germany with 95.7% of the vote and Austria with 98%—a mere eight months before his persecution of the Jews began. Had the vile dictator been honest about his intentions and motivations the landslide may well have been in the opposite direction, for people are repelled by dreams that are base, selfish, or petty, let alone evil. If your dream is about you—to become rich or powerful—others will not be inspired by it. The only people who will help you achieve it are those whose own motivation is to siphon away some of your wealth and power for themselves. Your dream must be about changing the world, helping others reach their potential, meeting a need, providing a service. A vision attracts others like a powerful magnet when it is perceived as noble and grand. But dishonorable ambitions emerge from a well polluted by small and self-centered thinking.

The word "vision," as it is used in this book, is not a carefully-crafted statement developed to focus your efforts or a sentence written on a business plan to unify your employees behind a common goal (though articulating these clearly can be helpful). Instead, your life vision is one that has already existed in your subconscious mind since childhood, and is being fleshed out daily in the circumstances of your life as an adult. Merely writing down a statement that is contrary to a destructive vision poisoning your well, therefore, is a frustrating exercise in futility. You might *consciously* set very high goals for yourself. You might even attend a seminar that inspires you to write those goals down, but until the message emerging from your well is in agreement with them, significant progress will be difficult.

In March of 1909, the American explorer Admiral Robert Peary was making his assault on the North Pole by dogsled. On one occasion he and his entourage hurried northward for an entire day, only to take their bearings and discover that they were further *south* than when they had begun that morning. Only later did he discover that he was traveling on a huge sheet of ice that had broken loose from the polar cap and was floating southward faster than his dogsled was traveling northward! His plight mirrors that of a person who is striving mightily to succeed, unaware that his subconscious mind, his vision of life, is pulling him toward failure at an even faster pace.

The conscious mind is incredibly small when compared to the subconscious one, like a solitary human being standing atop an ice sheet that is many miles across. In sheer proportions, the subconscious mind occupies many thousands of times more of our mental faculties than does the conscious mind. To make its dominance even more commanding, the subconscious mind labors 24 hours a day, while the conscious mind functions only while you are awake. The "ice sheet" of a negative life vision—if that is what you have—is pulling you backwards even when you are asleep! It should not surprise anyone, then, that substantial progress in a positive direction, which only occurs when you are awake and working, is almost impossible when your life vision is generally negative. The solution is not to travel faster while you are awake. That approach is futile and exhausting, doomed to failure from the start. The answer lies in changing your subconscious mind's vision of who you are and what you are to be and do. Peary's dilemma couldn't be solved by simply "mushing" faster; it could only be corrected by choosing to travel on ice that wasn't moving backwards to begin with. Better still would be to travel on a surface that is already moving in the direction you want to go. In this way, the potential *positive* influence of the subconscious mind can be just as astonishing as its negative effects.

The subconscious mind is never completely negative. It could never be completely anything. It is a hodgepodge of helpful, harmful, and neutral thoughts, memories, assumptions, feelings, and beliefs. Every piece of data that enters your mind through your five senses is recorded by your brain without regard for its accuracy or virtue. It is analyzed, sifted, interpreted, and either stored, ignored, rejected, or repressed. In this way, every bit of input, no matter how tiny or insignificant, changes you slightly. In the same way that anything dropped into a stew alters the composition and flavor of the whole pot, everything that goes into your well alters it slightly. Every bit of salt makes it saltier; every bit of sugar makes it sweeter. Therefore, just as the damaging beliefs dissolved in your well water never cease to exert their influence on you, the positive ones are also at work 24/7. Almost everyone has had the experience of going to bed at night with a vexing problem, only to awaken the following morning or in the middle of the night with a brilliant solution. We've all heard people respond to a challenging question by saying, "Let me sleep on it." In other words, they are saying, "Let me shut down my conscious mind and allow the creative genius of my subconscious to grapple with the issue."

Due to their contrast in size, your conscious mind is helpless to overcome the vision of life harbored in the subconscious. Day after day you may toil relentlessly to build the life you long for, but night after night the billions of neurons programmed for failure in your brain create a mysterious but overwhelming desire within you to sabotage your own success. Rigorous dieting is easily and predictably overcome by the irresistible urge to binge. Tireless efforts at the office are more than counteracted by the insatiable and bewildering need to challenge or antagonize the boss. Years of savings are swept away by gambling, drug, or alcohol habits. Great opportunities are ignored or squandered in an involuntary quest to confirm that it is the vision of life held in the subconscious mind that is accurate, not the more positive one nurtured in the conscious mind. Like a man trying to swim upstream in a strong current, the effort required for even small gains is enormous. To make matters worse, whenever he stops to rest all of his gains are rapidly erased. In this way, as the years go by, you will find yourself progressively further from your goals, having traveled "north" with all of your conscious energy, but somehow having found yourself afloat on a subconscious sheet of ice that is pulling you relentlessly backwards. How do you keep it all from "going south?"

Your subconscious vision of life may be revised, but the process is a long and difficult one. It is, however, well worth the effort. By reprogramming your subconscious mind, you can slowly stop the "southward" trend, and even reverse it. The benefits of accomplishing this are be enormous, because if you are successful in this endeavor you will find yourself moving *forward* even as you sleep! Eventually, the river in which you are swimming will start moving the same direction as your goals, amplifying your efforts instead of diminishing them, accelerating your pace rather than slowing it, buoying you up rather than weighing you down. This being the case, the challenging journey will pay abundant dividends in the end. Imagine your car, with the engine off, rolling slowly backwards. It is your task to stand behind the car, stop it and begin pushing it forward. Just getting the car to stop would require an enormous amount of effort. Starting it the opposite direction also calls for intense, backbreaking effort. But once the car is moving along the proper course, it begins to travel of its own momentum, requiring comparatively little effort on your part. Such is the job that awaits you as you attempt to reverse the direction of your life.

The subconscious mind is programmed by three factors:

1) The nature of the content it receives,

2) The frequency of that content, and

3) The *emotional impact* the messages create.

Assuming that you are willing to feed your brain uplifting content on a regular basis, the remaining necessary ingredient is *emotion*. Think for a moment about your earliest memories of life. Now think of more recent events, those from adolescence and beyond, that are the most vividly recorded in your memory. Chances are these memories were indelibly etched in your medial temporal lobe by powerful emotions. My only recollection of life as a toddler is burning my knee on our home furnace. I remember it because it was emotionally and physically traumatic. Had the furnace been off that day, I would have no memory of touching it at all. But as the imprint of the hot furnace grate was being physically seared into my tiny leg, the imprint of the event was simultaneously being seared into my memory by the fear, sadness, and sense of danger it created.

The clearest memories you have of childhood are probably those that caused you tremendous pain or great joy. You remember the other children teasing you; the broken leg at the playground; or the vicious scolding of a teacher, parent, or coach; or the death of a grandparent. Or, perhaps you remember receiving the bicycle you always wanted, or the arrival of a baby brother or sister, or moving into your family's new house. One of my clearest memories of childhood was watching as my best friend, five-year-old Peter, moving away. I stood in the middle of the street and stared as his face grew smaller and smaller in the rear window of his family's station wagon. Similarly, every strong emotion you experience has the potential of programming your subconscious mind. A child who is repeatedly teased or scolded is almost certain to find himself as an adult fighting a powerful current of negativity. The fortunate few whose childhood was almost an uninterrupted stream of positive reinforcement is likely to find success easy as an adult, for swimming with the current is a simple matter.

The events of our teen and adult years also tend to be those that are accompanied by strong feelings. We remember the weddings of those we loved dearly, but forget the unions of those we barely knew. The vows were similar, the ceremonies much alike, and the venues comparable. Why do we remember one, but not the other? Because we experienced strong emotions as we watched loved ones being wed. We easily recall the game or two in which our favorite team won or lost the championship, but can't remember the hundreds of games that were of little importance. We easily recall the deaths of those few people we knew well, and the moment we heard the tragic news is sometimes riveted in our memories, but we forget the hundreds of deaths of those we didn't love or didn't know. The circumstances are the same, yet the vividness of the memories remains starkly different; only the emotions associated with events causes one to stand out from all of the others in our memories. For this reason, the events that produced *powerful feelings* in you, whether positive or negative, are the ones whose impacts linger and resonate for decades in your subconscious mind. They are the seasonings that change the "flavor" of your well most profoundly, and once they are down in the well, they have no choice but to come up in the bucket.

At different stages of life, similar events might have markedly different emotional impacts on your psyche, because as you age your ability to properly evaluate those events improves. If someone called me stupid when I was a child, the words would cut deeply, cause me great anguish and likely flavor my well for many years to come. I might run home crying and stare in the mirror wondering why I was born so dense. I may angrily demand of God, "Why did you make me brainless?!??!" I might become anxiety-ridden before school exams, wondering if I could overcome my dullness. Even years later I might be hesitant to approach girls I found attractive, "knowing" that I would probably be rejected by them. After all, who would want to date a dimwit? I'd probably stumble all over myself and say something idiotic anyway, right? As an adult, however, I would respond to the same situation quite differently. If a colleague today told me I was stupid it might hurt my feelings slightly, but the event would not flavor my well much. Rather than crying and running away, I would simply shrug my shoulders and say, "Sorry you feel that way, but you're mistaken. I'm actually pretty smart." Why the difference? Because over the years I have received frequent, positive, and emotionally uplifting input regarding my intelligence. I've had many people tell me I'm smart, I did well in school, scored highly on I.Q. tests, and I've been successful at work. I've sensed the exhilaration of making perfect scores on tests that others in my class failed. I've experienced the satisfaction of graduating from two master's programs with honors. I've felt a sense of accomplishment after writing books and articles, and even been called brilliant on occasion. In other words, there is so much "sugar" already in my well (on that one issue, anyway) that a pinch of salt makes little difference. The water remains sweet.

As an adult, those events which are emotion-packed can actually *change the speed* of the ice sheet in your brain, whether it is traveling in the proper direction or not. If your life vision is one of failure and victimization, being fired from your job will tend to turbo-charge the ice sheet's southward flow. On the other hand, if you were to receive an unexpected promotion, the flow of the ice sheet would be slowed. However, since the current is already flowing in the wrong direction for most people, those events which *confirm* our damaging world view have a much more powerful influence than those which contradict it! To return to the car illustration, slowing down the backward roll of the car would require far more energy than merely increasing its speed in the wrong direction. In other words, standing in front of your moving car and pushing it in the (backward) direction it is already rolling would be easy. You could do it with one hand and little effort, giving it an occasional shove to help it on its way. However, standing behind it and *reversing* its direction is much more difficult. You would have to summon all your energy and strain mightily just to slow it down, fearing all the while that you might be steamrolled in the process. Herein lies the problem: there will probably never be enough positive events in the natural flow of your life to reverse your negative life vision. And since those vision-shaping events cannot be fully controlled anyway, *the key to reprogramming your brain is in finding a means of artificially manufacturing the powerful emotions that will help take your life where you want it to go.*

The subconscious mind responds to emotions, whether they are rooted in reality or not. Emotions felt deeply or consistently in your formative years imprint messages on your subconscious mind, even if they do not accurately reflect the truth. Those messages play back over and over again through adult life, long after you discover that the events that produced them were childish misunderstandings. For example, a small girl who grows up believing she is physically unattractive will—even after blossoming into a beautiful young woman—still tend to feel insecure in social situations. When she looks in the mirror she will invariably see tiny blemishes, invisible to others, which reinforce her belief that she is ugly. When a potential suitor delays in returning her phone calls, she imagines that it is because she is undesirable, and her ice sheet accelerates slightly. Her mother and friends may tell her that she is lovely, but these messages are insufficient to change her vision of herself. A man might tell her she is attractive, but she will dismiss the compliment as empty flattery. After all, she has a mirror, doesn't she? She "knows" in her own mind that she is ugly, even if objectively this is not the case. What will it take to convince her otherwise?

If a long series of men begin to treat her as though she is quite attractive, she will eventually begin to doubt the objectivity of her own assessment of her looks. Once this occurs, these men might be able to make her *feel* beautiful, and the ice sheet will gradually come to a halt and even reverse direction. Ideally, truth should seep into all of our minds this way. However, the scenario just described is unlikely to happen to anyone who is not exceptionally good-looking, so very few people will receive enough positive input to create this natural change in vision. Yet, by artificially and intentionally implanting the same emotions in our minds, the vision will change nonetheless.

I call the process of reversing your life vision "Emotionation." This term is derived from combining the words emotion and imagination, and aptly so because those are the two ingredients necessary to transform your vision of yourself and your world. Your subconscious mind received messages when you were a child, ones that later proved to be false: "No one loves me," "I'm stupid," "I can't do anything right." Yet their impact lingers to this day. Since your mind so readily received false messages back then, it stands to reason that it will continue to receive them today as well, even if their impact is not as profound. When you were a child, the feelings that programmed your brain were triggered by events, words, and circumstances that were beyond your control. As an adult, however, you have much more control over the messages that enter your mind, and how deeply they penetrate your psyche.

Emotionation is achieved when you deliberately imagine an event so vividly that you feel the same emotions you would experience if the imagined situations had actually occurred. A man who won the Heisman Trophy or a woman who was crowned Miss America would undoubtedly experience such positive emotions that their confidence level would be enhanced for decades to come. But the fact that only one man and one woman receive those honors each year need not prevent you from enjoying the same benefits, because vividly imagining similar positive events programs the inner workings of your brain in much the same way! Through a carefully-planned series of mental exercises occupying no more than a few minutes each day, you can bring your life vision (the one forced on you by circumstances when you were a child) into line with your life dream (the goals you most want to achieve).

Emotionation is accomplished by envisioning with great concentration the success you desire. You need only invest two or three minutes per day in this effort. Sit alone in a comfortable chair, close your eyes, and focus intensely on the outcome you long for. Reduce your goal to a single brief sentence and repeat it silently until you experience the exhilaration that should come with success. Then recall the greatest defeats or rejections you have experienced, but imagine them turning out completely differently. The goal of this practice is to attempt to erase the negative influence those events have had on your brain. Once you begin to feel elation and excitement as though your goals have already been achieved, your subconscious mind will absorb them and start the long process of slowing the southward flow of your ice sheet. While the change will be initially imperceptible, over months of repeating this exercise their combined impact will make a noticeable difference in your confidence level and, therefore, your behavior. As the ice sheet slows, your progress will accelerate. When it finally stops and reverses direction, you will be headed for great success and the fulfillment of your vision.

Chapter III

AN ATTITUDE
OF STEADY PROGRESS

Happy people have a sense that they are making measurable progress toward their goals. At any point, they can look back at the previous few weeks and months and see that their actions have brought them closer to fulfilling their dreams, and this evidence of steady progress becomes a source of deep satisfaction and encouragement to them. Conversely, those who look back at the past year and see no discernible progress toward their dreams carry an unavoidable sense of wasted time, regret, and hopelessness. Like a car stuck in the mud, they spin their wheels furiously but to no avail. In this regard, the path to success and the path to happiness are one and the same: steady movement toward a worthy goal.

The definition of a worthy goal is simple: a worthy goal is any objective that is important *to you*. With the notable exception of your boss, who has every right to impose some of the company's goals on you, no one should be allowed to establish *your* goals. In order to be happy, you must decide which objectives are worthy of your time and commitment. Your goal might be to become a scratch golfer, or visit every country of the world, or be the best grandparent on earth, or save a million dollars, or pay off your mortgage, or over-throw a small nation! Or it might be to become the CEO of your company, write a book, or just to *read* a book! Regard-less of what you choose to do with your life, it is essential that you write your aims down, because there is *nothing* that you can do with less time, talent, energy, commitment, or fewer resources that will change your life more than writing down specific goals and reading them regularly.

I have carried with me for many years a list of about 160 items that I would like to achieve. It was my "bucket list" three decades before the term was created. Some of the items on the list are grandiose, others are mundane. While some will take years to achieve, others can be completed in an afternoon. Goals range from financial independence to learning to ride a unicycle. Prominent on the list are attending important sporting events like the Super Bowl, the NCAA Men's Basketball Final Four, and the NBA Finals. Other notable entries include places I would like to visit: the Eiffel Tower, the Great Wall of China, the Taj Mahal, the Acropolis, the Great Barrier Reef, and the Pyramids of Egypt. Dozens of other items on the list describe personal interests: learning to waltz, having a speaking part in a motion picture, watching a rocket launch from the Kennedy Space Center, etc. Beside each item on the list is a box that I can check as I accomplish each one. Regularly checking off these items makes me happy. Going months without accomplishing a single one brings me sadness.

The most challenging goals on the list require continual effort almost every day over many months or years. Such objectives must be broken down into many tiny goals that can serve as milestones as you travel toward the ultimate destination. There is an old adage that I have expanded and modified into a short poem:

> *"Mile by mile life's a difficult trial;*
>
> *Even yard by yard it's hard.*
>
> *A foot at a time's still a challenging climb,*
>
> *But inch by inch it's a cinch!"*

Almost everyone has at least a few grand dreams, but the dreamers who actually achieve their goals are not mere dreamers; they are also *doers.* Zig Ziglar, perhaps the world's best-known motivator, has often said, "The difference between a dreamer and achiever is that the achiever knows how to break his dreams down into daily steps." This comprises one of the great secrets of highly successful people: *They take baby steps every day toward their dreams.* They save small amounts of money regularly, they write a paragraph or page each day on the dreamt-of bestseller, they hammer or saw or sand a few minutes each day to transform their fixer-upper into a mansion. They study management or sales or customer service books regularly until they have mastered the skills that will be needed to fulfill their dreams.

I developed a simple tool to force me to take such tiny steps toward my goals. I call it my "Life Template." I listed on a half-sheet of paper ten areas of my life in which I want to make steady progress toward lifetime goals. An example is printed below so that you will easily be able to make your own and customize it to your situation.

MARRIAGE: _____

PARENTING: _____

CAREER: _____

SPANISH: _____

MAGIC: _____

HEALTH: _____

WRITING: _____

MARKETING: _____

CHARITY: _____

Whenever I feel that I am losing my focus or failing to make progress, I take out one of these "Life Templates" and simply write one small item in the blank beside each category that I plan to do *that day* to make progress toward my goals. Beside "Marriage" I might write, "Buy flowers for my wife." Next to "Parenting" I would scribble, "Take my son to the park." In the "Career" blank I would make a note to make a phone call I've been putting off to someone who could be of help to my career. I would then open my Spanish dictionary (Becoming fluent in Spanish is a goal of mine.) and write down a word that I don't know in the "Spanish" blank, pledging to memorize its meaning by day's end. Alongside "Magic" I would write down "Practice new coin trick," because as a professional illusionist I must improve constantly. The list will vary for each person, but the ultimate effect it will have on your life will be the same.

The Toyota car company is a wonderful example of this principle. Founded in Japan in 1957, its first car was a flop. The "Corona," as it was called, was a model of fuel efficiency, but struggled to reach 60 miles per hour. Top executives at Toyota responded by implementing a philosophy they called "Kaizen," which means "continuous improvement." They resolved that each automobile they built would be an improvement on previous ones. Within two decades they had secured their hold within the automobile industry in the fuel efficiency niche, delivering the Carina, the Celica, the Camry and the Corolla. Now Toyota vehicles are recognized as rivaling the best in the world, all due to relentless, steady progress toward their goal.

Most people, however, remain passive while hoping and praying for an unforeseen windfall to rescue them from mediocrity. Rather than taking the bull by the horns and proactively pursuing their goals inch by inch, they fantasize that a sudden "big break" will result in fame, status, or wealth. In reality, however, only a tiny fraction of the world's wealthy and powerful attained their status via a windfall from a lottery, lawsuit, sweepstakes, or inheritance. The vast majority got there by a very different strategy: the *slight edge*. By outworking or out-earning others by a tiny amount each day, you will gradually pull ahead and move steadily toward your goals. Let's use financial success as an example, since it is so much easier to quantify and measure than other types of goals.

Those who are wealthy usually got that way by thinking like wealthy people, and therefore engaging in behaviors that eventually produce wealth. They save their money and invest it, counting on interest for a portion of their income growth. They outwork their competition, often starting their own businesses so that they have no externally-imposed limit to their income. They pay off their credit card bills in full each month, thus avoiding the exorbitant interest that would otherwise accrue. They spend wisely, and seek to use their money on purchases that will generate income or appreciate in value. They live within their means so that they will always have money to spare. Most wealthy people are wealthy because they spend a lifetime doing the things wealthy people do. These behaviors emerge from the wellspring of accurate beliefs about wealth, just as the choices of the poor originate in the murky waters of their tainted wells.

The presence or absence of monetary riches is usually evidence of a proper or improper way of thinking about money that existed long before. This explains why wealthy people who suddenly lose their money to a lawsuit, a change in the market, the collapse of the economy, or theft usually become wealthy again. Similarly, when a poor person suddenly becomes wealthy as the result of a lawsuit or lottery win, the money seldom lasts. Though the bank account balance has changed, the mindset has remained the same. For both the suddenly rich and the suddenly broke the habits acquired over a lifetime slowly take over and cause the newly poor to grow wealthy again, and the suddenly rich to return to their poverty. Perhaps this is why Mahatma Gandhi believed that unearned money was one of only a handful of genuine evils.

Compounding the problem for the suddenly rich person is the internal mirror that portrays him or her as a poor person masquerading as a rich one. The appearance of stability and self-assurance provided by wealth feels like a mere facade concealing deep-seated feelings of insecurity, guilt, and unworthiness. Rather than remaking the old house, they have simply given it a new coat of paint. Below the beautiful new veneer, the same termites of under-confidence, the dry rot of fear, and the decay of slothfulness remain, eating their way back to the surface. Slowly but surely, their poor self-image begets self-destructive behaviors intended by their subconscious mind to return them to the quagmire of debt and poverty they secretly view as their rightful place in society. The ice sheet continues south even if the dogsled has been traded in for a Ferrari.

The belief that sudden wealth is the answer to most of life's problems is almost universal. However, its widespread appeal doesn't make it true. In fact, sudden wealth frequently makes financial problems even worse, because it serves merely to magnify the character flaws that existed long before the windfall. People who are poor became that way by handling money foolishly, or by living with someone who does. They *think* like poor people, and therefore will inevitably sink into a morass of financial struggle or even destitution. A lifetime of choices to spend their money on lottery tickets (the state of Illinois reported in September, 2002 that the average citizen of that state spends $500 per year on lottery tickets!), or alcohol, or drugs, or questionable investments ensures that they will never have money to spare. By ending their education too soon, failing to discipline themselves, and engaging in impulse buying they have established a financial glass ceiling over their own heads. By failing to understand that profits are much to be preferred to wages they have entrenched themselves in a no-higher-than-middle-class existence. They purchase items they can't afford (often at outrageous interest rates) in order to impress others. They then make the minimum payment each month on their credit cards. *Poor people are poor because they (or someone close to them, such as a spouse or parent) have spent a lifetime doing the things that poor people do.* Merely winning the lottery does not change these behaviors; quite the contrary, it amplifies them.

A sudden windfall does not reverse the poverty-bound ice flow in the winner's brain; on the contrary, it accelerates it. The spend-more-than-you-have mentality still exists, merely emboldened by the sudden influx of cash. A person with no money in savings who owed $20,000 on credit cards prior to the financial boon will soon be likely to have $500,000 in the bank and owe $1,000,000! The poor man who once spent his meager disposable income on booze can now afford to fully stock a personal in-home bar and is likely to parlay his bad habit into full-blown alcoholism. The occasional recreational drug user can now afford enough cocaine to destroy or even end his life. The over-spender can now bankrupt herself with risky investments and outrageous purchases, and now breathlessly sits up all night watching the Home Shopping Network with a telephone in one hand and Master-Card® in the other. The party animal who was once a fixture at other people's social gatherings now hosts his own galas with expensive bands, free-flowing booze, lavish catered dinners, and drugs free-for-the-taking. Dangerous behaviors that were once enjoyed in comparatively safe moderation are given free rein to destroy the suddenly wealthy. This is why winning the lottery is more often an evil than a good. In fact, the *New York Post* reported in 1997 that fully one-third of all state lottery winners eventually file for bankruptcy!

Far from solving all problems, sudden wealth generally creates a predicament of mammoth proportions, creating internal stress, fomenting family conflicts, and attracting an onslaught of gold-diggers. A person who prior to the windfall made thirty-five thousand dollars per year, but owed $150,000 on a home, car, and credit cards typically learns the hard way that great riches only multiply their problems. They soon discover that possessing one million dollars merely enables them to incur debts of multiple millions. Dubbed "affluenza" by those who have studied the effects of sudden wealth, this disease flows into the tiny cracks in the winner's soul and hardens there, deepening them, widening them, exposing and exploiting them. What the "winner" believed was his or her key to happiness often opens the door to despair. The unexpected riches serve only to unleash and magnify the weaknesses of the recipient, who was previously restrained in his or her excess, even if only by the lack of money. An abrupt increase in wealth simply removes a major obstacle to dissipation, debauchery, and recklessness, clearing the path to self-destruction.

An article in a British newspaper, the *Sunday Mercury*, once chronicled the demise of many of that country's lottery winners. A carpenter won 1.8 million British pounds in 1999, moved into a mansion, became a recluse, and drank himself to death. A friend said of his final days, "For the last six weeks of his life, he existed on whiskey." A 39 year-old father of three won 2.1 million pounds and died of a heart attack, apparently from the stress of his win, less than two years later. Another man, Roy Wilson, won 1.1 million pounds and was immediately embroiled in a family dispute about how the winnings would be distributed in the event of his death (he was 57). The family feared that Wilson's partner, Denise Hanson, 52, would get all the money. The stress associated with his win apparently contributed to his untimely demise, and a legal nightmare ensued. One of his four children squandered his share of the inheritance in five months on drugs, then was jailed for breaking into his sister's home in search of more money to fund his heroin addiction. His sister, Donna, said, "I hate what the lottery has done to this family. People think it brings happiness, but it has ruined our lives."

The results in America have been similar. A 1988 book by Jerry Dennis chronicled the stories of lottery winners in Michigan. *Money for Nothing* describes how tax troubles, poor investments, and family pressures have ruined the lives of some so-called winners. Relatives began to call and beg for money to get them out of debt, or to pay for their operations, or to buy new houses. "It's not like you earned the money, you know!" they shout. "It could have been me that won the money just as easily as you!" "I'd give you some if I were in your shoes!" Eventually, many recipients of sudden unearned wealth are forced to sever family ties and long-standing friendships altogether and move to another city for a fresh start. But once again, the supposed "fresh start" is really not a solution. It is merely a relocation of the same old bad habits and misunderstandings that caused financial struggles before the lottery win.

Such winners often quit their jobs and try to spend their way to happiness. Along the way, they usually discover that they had been deceiving themselves all those years that they insisted they hated their jobs. They start to dislike waking up with nothing to do. They lose their sense of purpose and begin to miss their coworkers and careers. They sleep until ten every morning, watch a couple of game shows, and then putter around the house wishing they had a reason to live. They discover that their new wealth does not buy happiness. Rather, it purchases the anesthetic of toys, trips, and parties that temporarily deadens the pain and distracts them from the emptiness and depression that now threaten to swallow them.

Jack Whittaker, the flamboyant West Virginian who became instantly famous on Christmas Day, 2002 by winning $170 million dollars playing Powerball, is another example. After taxes, he took home a check for $114 million. But the kind-hearted gentleman's life quickly degenerated. Armed with ready cash, the devout church-goer became a fixture at local strip clubs and was known for dropping huge tips on the dancers. Months later, thieves broke into his car where it was parked at "The Pink Pony" and made off with almost $550,000 in cash. A few months later his car was again robbed, this time of $100,000. Three of his granddaughter's boyfriends were arrested and convicted of the crime. Teenage Brandi, Jack's only grandchild, was "my whole world," he liked to say. But she lost all of her friends after the lottery win, concluding all they wanted was money. She became bitter, "the most bitter 17-year-old I've ever seen," Jack said, and was found dead later that year of an overdose of hard illegal drugs—drugs paid for by her grandfather's windfall. In a devastating twist of fate, she was buried on Christmas Eve, just one day short of the two-year anniversary of the lottery win. Jack was then sued by an Atlantic City casino for bouncing $1.5 million in checks written to cover his gambling debts. He was twice arrested for driving while intoxicated, and pleaded no contest to charges that he attacked a bar manager. He was ordered to attend weekly Alcoholics Anonymous meetings, and was later sentenced to one month in a rehabilitation clinic. He was reported to be drinking heavily and paying women huge sums for sex. He was spotted cavorting with a woman who was not his wife. He renovated a secluded house with a Charleston woman and spent time with her there. While in the love nest awaiting Jack's arrival one day the mistress was robbed at gunpoint of $25,000. His wife, Jewell, who had been Jack's love since the eighth grade, filed for divorce in 2005. He has been involved in over 450 lawsuits or legal actions since the win. Eleven of his employees have been indicted for embezzling his money. In 2006, robbers took an enormous, though undisclosed, amount of his money by scamming 12 branches of the bank that held his winnings. In 2007, he claimed he was broke. In 2009, Jack's only child Ginger, Brandi's mother, died of a drug overdose. Jewell Whittaker's assessment of her husband's lottery win was this: "If I'd known what was going to transpire, honestly, I would have torn the ticket up."

Sudden wealth is rarely a cure. "Get rich quick" is a pipe dream for fools; "get rich slow and steady" is the mantra of the wise. Far superior is the slow, relentless accumulation of wealth achieved by wise choices and personal discipline over a period of many years. Albert Einstein once said, "The greatest mystery on earth is compounded interest." Indeed a small investment made early in life grows at a geometric rate, imperceptibly at first, then a little more, then by leaps and bounds. Money invested at only a 10% annual return doubles in just over seven years. It doubles the original amount again in only four years, and again in two-and-a-half years. As the money grows, so does the person who owns it, and the values and behaviors that produced it are internalized, strengthened and reinforced. *What is true of money is also true of actions.* Sensible behaviors relentlessly pursued year after year often create little visible difference in the short term, but in the long run the contrast is astounding. Happy people make it a priority to work daily on their goals, even if the progress made seems tiny and insignificant.

Wise people recognize that they do not have to work twice as hard as others to excel. Nor do they need to merely hope and pray to be plucked from obscurity and given a position of prominence in the business world, onstage, or on the silver screen. On the contrary, they recognize that they need *only work three or four percent harder and longer* over a period of years to eventually obtain a huge advantage. An automobile traveling 61 miles per hour for eight hours will only travel eight miles further than one traveling 60. But if this tiny difference is maintained over the course of a month, the gap is widened to 240 miles. In a year, the slightly faster car has opened a nearly 3000 mile lead, and in ten years has traveled more than the entire circumference of the globe farther than the one traveling only a tiny bit slower.

Jay Leno, host of NBC's *The Tonight Show with Jay Leno*, seemed to be in deep trouble in 1993 when David Letterman made the jump to CBS to compete directly with him. Letterman was clearly winning the ratings war, but slowly Leno crept into contention, overtook him in 1995, and then won soundly for the next several years. His secret? Leno attributes his victory to his dogged perseverance, his determination to simply outwork the competition every single day. By spending his entire adult life working when his opponents were vacationing, resting, or recreating he slowly but steadily overtook and beat them out. Leno once told *People* magazine, "When I was a kid growing up ... I had dyslexia. My mother told me that I would always have to work twice as hard as the other kids just to get the same grades. It's the same now. I'm not better than anybody else doing this job;

I just think maybe I work harder than some." Rather than passively waiting for a "big break" to rescue him, he simply outworked the competition by a small margin over a period of years. His "big break" did not come suddenly. It was the result of thousands of hours of relentless effort. As the great poet, Henry Wadsworth Longfellow, wrote:

The heights by great men reached and kept

Were not attained by sudden flight,

But they, while their companions slept,

Were toiling upward in the night.

America's greatest president, Abraham Lincoln, toiled away each night studying and worked tirelessly each day to build his legal practice. His described his work ethic this way: "I walk slowly, but I never walk backward." That is the key! Place one foot in front of the other, day after day, week after week, decade after decade, plodding persistently forward, never sideways or backwards, choosing the way of the tortoise rather than that of the hare. Lincoln's genius was that of the plodder, not the sprinter. Your approach should be the same.

For many, the key to great success will be a simple decision to work two hours longer each week, to make one additional sales call each day, to watch one less television program each evening, to rise thirty minutes earlier each morning, or exercise one more time per week. One additional date with your spouse each month can turn a marriage around. An extra twenty minutes daily with your child can cement your relationship for life. Three less soft drinks consumed each week can slim your waistline and lengthen your life. The Apostle Paul, in the book of Galatians, wrote the following words:

"Let us not grow weary in well-doing, for in due season we will reap, if we do not give up." He was singing the praises of the plodder, one who merely walks slowly forward day after day after day, knowing that progress is being made even if it is so tiny as to be unseen by others.

Chapter IV

AN ATTITUDE
OF INTEGRITY

"Honesty is the first chapter in the book of wisdom." So said Thomas Jefferson. As it turns out, honesty is also the first chapter in the book of happiness and long-term success, because character correlates strongly with both. Despite the sometimes strong temptation to get ahead by lying, cheating, and stealing, lasting fulfillment can rarely be gained dishonestly. Even those who appear to have succeeded by other-than-honest means rarely meet with a happy end. Quite the opposite, their lives tend to slowly degenerate as they become victims of what I call "The Law of Integrity." The Law of Integrity states that you cannot cheat yourself into happiness any more than you can drink yourself into sobriety. Working almost as consistently as gravity, the Law of Integrity applies a downward pull on those who take ethical shortcuts to get what they want, eventually bringing them back to earth with a deafening crash.

I am convinced that every violation of your integrity will ultimately make you a less-happy person. Furthermore, cheating will—over the course of the years—undermine your success, as well. If my thesis is correct, every lie that you tell (with the exception of the harmless encouraging compliments we pay people daily to make them feel good or avoid hurting their feelings), every personal long-distance call you make on the company phone, every ill-gotten dollar you gain and every overage on your expense invoice will, in the end, diminish your happiness. This is because when decent people engage in dishonorable behaviors, they begin to respect themselves less. Their opinion of themselves is lowered. If you violate your integrity often enough, you will slowly descend into self-loathing. This decrease in your self-esteem will gradually make you less effective, less confident, less joyful, and usually less successful, as well.

I have often compared each person's individual search for happiness to a trip in a rowboat. Each of us rows about on the vast lake that is our lifespan, crossing paths with others, peering into other people's boats in search of that missing something that we can put in our own boat to make us happy. As a small child, I row over to Mommy and say, "If you would throw a little approval my way that would float my boat." Then I row over to Daddy and say, "A new bicycle would really float my boat." In high school, I maneuver my way to the coach and say, "If you would put me on the team that would float my boat." Then in college I encounter someone I think is cute and say, "If we could row side by side for a while, that would *really* float my boat." Later, we say to that same person, "Why don't you just get in my boat with me and we'll row through life together?" And, of course, you make the discovery that not only does marriage not float your boat, it drills holes in your boat! Then children come along like torpedoes and knock the bottom right out of it! And over a period of years and decades, many of the things we acquired in hopes of floating our boat actually become sources of strain and anxiety. A similar leak develops in our souls when we violate the law of integrity.

Each spring, millions of Americans are tempted to cheat on their income tax returns. This almost universal temptation results from a flawed reasoning process which concludes, "If I underreport my income to the IRS, I'll get to keep an extra few hundred dollars this year, and that will float my boat." And as you may expect, that extra few hundred dollars might indeed bring a small measure of happiness and "float your boat" for a while, but the act of gaining the money dishonestly also drills a hole in the hull. Long after the money has been spent, the hole will remain. And with each dishonest act you will have sentenced yourself to live many years with the memory of what you've done wrong. The pangs of conscience and lowered self-esteem are compounded with each deceitful act, and over the course of many years the *integrity* of the hull is being compromised by those who would try to cheat their way into a fulfilled life.

In my act as a traveling professional magician I usually do a routine that uses milk, and performing the routine almost always gets my hands wet. For this reason, before each show I borrow a hand towel from my hotel room. Over many years, I have dutifully returned the towel to the hotel after each show, sometimes driving miles out of my way to do so. However, several years ago I was hastily packing up my show in a harried attempt to get to the airport in time for my flight home. Some of my props were damp as the result of the milk illusion and I didn't have time to dry them properly. And so I rationalized. I reasoned, "This hotel has *thousands* of towels. They couldn't possibly miss just one of them. Besides, I've been so careful all these years to return hundreds of these towels, that I can't really be blamed for taking just one." I quickly wrapped the wet items with the towel, closed my footlocker, and hopped in a taxi. Now, every time I open that footlocker to prepare for a new show, I see that towel and a tiny wave of remorse sweeps over me. I think to myself, "I can't believe that I am the type of person who would steal a towel from a hotel." I can't even mail it back to them because I've forgotten which hotel it was! By taking what wasn't mine, I have condemned myself to live the rest of my life with the knowledge that I traded my integrity for a used hand towel! The gain of one small towel pales in significance compared to the regret I feel for having drilled a small hole in the hull of my own boat.

The word "integrity" is derived from the mathematical term "integer," referring to a whole number (that is, a number with no fractions). Integrity, then, refers to a person who is 100% of something, with nothing added or taken away. The integrity of a ship's hull is said to have been breached when a crack or hole exists, because it is no longer uniform throughout; that is, it is no longer 100% intact. When speaking to teenagers I have often illustrated this point by holding up several candy bars: a Butterfinger, Mounds, Hershey Bar, Almond Joy, Payday, 100 Grand, etc. I then make the assertion that only one of the bars has integrity, asking for the young people to guess which one and why. It surprises me that no one has ever been able to do so successfully. The correct answer is the Hershey Bar, because it is the only one that is *the same all the way through*. The others are a combination of nuts, chocolate, nougat, peanut butter, caramel, etc. But a Hershey Bar is *pure* chocolate. Every bite is exactly the same as every other. If you cut it into a thousand tiny pieces, each one would be identical in makeup to all of the others. A person with integrity, likewise, is the same on the inside as he or she is on the outside. They are the same person in public that they are in private.

Similarly, the word "sincere" is a combination of two Latin words which mean "without wax." In ancient times, dishonest potters would try to sell damaged clay pots to unsuspecting customers by filling the cracks with wax before painting them. Once heated, of course, the wax would melt and the pots would become useless. To combat this unscrupulous practice, Roman inspectors were required to examine pottery before it was sold and mark it *"sine cere,"* without wax. Once again, the emphasis is that a "sincere" pot was 100% clay, with no concealed flaws. The *integrity* of the vessel was certified. So it is with a sincere person, as well. There are no pretenses, no façades and no false fronts. Contrast this with the words we use to describe a person who *lacks* integrity.

If integrity refers to oneness then the lack thereof is, as you might expect, expressed by the exact *opposite* of uniformity. There are many metaphors which illustrate this principle. The Native Americans (in old movies, if not in reality) derided deceitful white people as speaking "with a forked tongue." A politician who tells one group of constituents one thing and another group something entirely different is engaging in "doubletalk." We refer to a dishonest person as being "two-faced," and criticize hypocrites as "double-dealers." A person who promises you one thing but does another is said to have "double-crossed" you. We describe insincere people as "speaking out of both sides of their mouths." Even the word "duplicitous" comes from the Latin word for "double," the antithesis of someone with oneness, integrity. A man who cheats on his girlfriend is a "two-timer." In each case the oneness of integrity has been replaced by a duality. Instead of a person who is of one uniform nature throughout, he is an individual who is part one thing, part another. Happiness for the dishonest person is very elusive, for the person who is part clay, part wax will leak joy in the same way that a compromised pot leaks water.

Dishonesty not only diminishes your own view of yourself, it also lowers the esteem other people have for you. Imagine the difficulty of regaining the trust of someone whom you have deceived. Many a marriage has taken years to recover from one lie, and many more are ended altogether for the same reason. Family relationships can be devastated by insincerity or dishonesty. Consider the challenge of trying to regain a customer that you have cheated (almost impossible), and the damage done to your reputation in the marketplace. One shady deal intended to net you an extra few thousand dollars can cost you many tens of thousands in lost business before the hemorrhaging can be stanched. The loss of business and personal relationships will far outweigh, in the long run, any short-term gain as the law of integrity takes its toll.

Integrity is very hard to maintain; it is incredibly easy to lose. Years of honest decisions can be outweighed by a single act of deceit. Though it seems horribly unfair, your character is often judged either by a lifetime of consecutive good decisions or by one isolated bad one. A man who is faithful to his wife 364 days per year, yet strays on

December 31st, is not considered 99.73% faithful, but 100% unfaithful. A banker who spends 19 years meticulously handling money, yet embezzles $10,000 in the 20th is not considered to be 95% employable in the financial sector, but 100% unemployable. Like a piece of glass, once broken it cannot be restored. It may be patched or glued, or the sharp edges dulled and weathered by the years, but the scar remains and the value of the glass is forever impaired. The best you can hope for is to sever all relationships, move away, and start again with an unsullied reputation. But even then, the fear of being discovered remains.

When you forfeit your integrity, you must then divert mental and emotional energy to cover up your lies. Those who know the truth must be kept away from those who don't. Cover stories must be conceived and delivered without slip-up. For example, a husband or wife who is having an affair is seldom fully focused on any task at hand. Almost every word that is spoken must be evaluated before it passes through the lips, lest a telltale secret be accidentally revealed. Actions and reactions and alibis and bogus explanations must be preplanned and rehearsed. Like Bobby Fisher engrossed in a chess match, the unfaithful spouse spends agonizing hours considering every conceivable eventuality, and the potential implications of every possible permutation of each imaginable occurrence. Sleep is lost as contingencies are formulated, and contingencies to contingencies, and contingencies to those contingencies, and valuable mental resources are siphoned away from work and legitimate relationships to maintain the façade, not to mention the hours of productive work lost to the affair itself. Years ago I was waiting to deliver the keynote address at a corporate conference while that company's CEO made some introductory remarks. As he spoke to his employees he shared his philosophy of life. He said, "In order to be really happy, a man needs a wife, a lover, and a best friend. And if those three are all the same person, it sure saves a lot of time!" Given the reality of the "slight edge principle" in the preceding chapter, dishonesty can be the difference between success and failure *even if the lie is never exposed*, for the time lost to the affair and its cover-up may transform your slight edge into an ever-growing deficit.

Perhaps never before has ethics in business occupied such a prominent place in the national psyche. Corporate scandals hatched in the 1990s ate away at the foundations of major American corporations and burst onto the front pages of the newspapers in the first few years of the new century. It is difficult to imagine better examples of the how the law of integrity applies to businesses than the negative consequences of deceit experienced by the offending companies and their executives. Former Adelphia Communications CEO John Rigas, along with his son Timothy, misused their positions to conceal $2.3 billion in debt, while embezzling $100 million in cash to cover their own personal investment losses and pay for luxury condos and a golf course. Their lifestyles were extravagant and enviable... until the law of integrity exacted its toll. Their actions brought about the collapse of the nation's fifth largest cable company. In April, 2004, the men agreed to forfeit 95% of their financial assets. Three months later, both men were sentenced to long prison terms.

About that same time, Tyco CEO Dennis Kozlowski and his CFO, Mark Schwartz, were convicted by a New York jury for looting the company of $600 million dollars. Prosecutors had cited a lavish $2 million birthday party

Kozlowski held for his wife on the Italian island of Sardinia, and a $6,000 shower curtain he had paid for with company funds, among many other such extravagances as proof of his larceny. They were fined a collective $239 million dollars, and both received a sentence of 8.5 to 25 years in prison for their crimes. Kozlowski's salary at Tyco was $300 million dollars in his final year at the helm; now he reportedly makes $74 a week working in the prison laundry at Midstate Correctional Institution near Rome, New York.

A year later, Worldcom CEO Bernard Ebbers was sentenced to 25 years in prison for perpetrating the largest accounting fraud in the country's history ($11 billion!). Thousands of investors were intentionally defrauded, the court ruled, and hundreds of WorldCom employees were laid off in the scandal. Ebbers was forced to relinquish $45 million in assets, including a mansion in Mississippi. His wife was allowed to keep a modest home in Jackson, along with $50,000. A 63-year-old man at the time of his conviction, Ebbers will likely spend the remainder of his life behind bars.

The names Andrew Fastow, Jeffrey Skilling, and Kenneth Lay, all top executives at Enron, will undoubtedly go down in history as the poster-children of corporate fraud. The men were all convicted of multiple counts of fraud involving an elaborate scheme to conceal massive losses in offshore dummy-companies while publicly declaring the company to be healthy and profitable. Thousands of Enron employees lost their life savings in the debacle, while tens of thousands of investors saw their stock drop in value from $90.56 in August of 2000 to a mere fifty cents per share in December of 2001. One employee described how he had helplessly watched his retirement account plunge from $1.3 million to

$8,000. The rank-and-file employees were forbidden to sell their shares, while executives dumped theirs. Two of the primary perpetrators, along with several other lesser offenders, will spend many years in prison. Kenneth Lay, himself, died shortly after his conviction, almost certainly from the stress caused by the scandal. To make matters worse, the storied accounting firm Arthur Andersen was all but destroyed in the same scandal, though its conviction was overturned by the Supreme Court on a technicality.

The granddaddy of all swindles in the first decade of this new century was perpetrated by Bernard Madoff. Over a 30-year "career" Madoff and a few associates erected a $65 billion dollar Ponzi scheme that finally came crashing down in December of 2008. Bilking celebrities, universities, investment firms, private investors, and even charities, he lived a life of opulence on the backs of his unsuspecting dupes. He apparently hid the scam even from his own family, who now bear the shame of a last name that has become synonymous with fraud. His elder son, Mark, hanged himself two years to the day after his father's arrest. Bernie Madoff, himself, will spend the remainder of his life in prison at Butner Federal Correctional Institute near Raleigh, North Carolina, an eight-hour drive from his family in New York. Ironically, he shares the prison with John and Timothy Rigas.

Similar scandals have engulfed HealthSouth Corporation, Rite Aid Corporation, and Lucent Technologies. In Japan, the former president of Mitsubishi, Takashi Usami, along with ten other top executives went to jail as a result of a carefully orchestrated strategy to hide defects in one of their truck models, a flaw in the drive shaft that resulted in the death of a 39-year-old man. In years past, America has watched the meteoric rise and sobering collapse of men like Ivan Boesky, Michael Milken, and Charles Keating. Each man and company described above serves to confirm that the law of integrity cannot be defied. Like the law of gravity, it cannot be broken; you can only be broken upon it.

Fortunately, this law also helps those who obey it. Those who discipline themselves to be honest and forthcoming in all of their business dealings develop a reputation for trustworthiness. Customers return again and again, knowing that they will not be cheated, but will be treated fairly. A 2006 study revealed that companies deemed to be the most ethical in the country outperformed their competitors in the S&P 500 by 370% over five years. The Institute of Business Ethics in Great Britain released a similar report in 2003. It revealed that the stock price of ethical companies was far less volatile than that of unethical ones. Ethosphere magazine's 2010 list of the 100 most ethical companies in America showed that while the other 400 presumably less ethical companies in the S&P 500 saw a 4% decrease in stock price, the moral leaders saw an average increase of 53%. The clear conclusion is that the more ethical a business is, the more profitable it tends to be, as well. It seems reasonable, then, that the same would be true of an individual.

Each violation of your integrity drills one more hole in your boat, opens one more fissure in your clay pot. Over the span of many years, you are either maintaining a vessel whose integrity is largely intact, or you are developing a sieve. If it is the latter, you are doomed to arrive in your old age as a bitter old man or woman, leaking happiness faster than you can possibly replenish it, or taking on sorrow faster than you can bail it out. If, on the other hand, you have maintained your integrity, you are very likely to have a smooth boat ride through your golden years. Your pot will be filled to the rim with joy, and anything poured into it will simply cause it to overflow with more happiness.

Chapter V

AN ATTITUDE
OF INTIMACY

Every individual has the same ultimate goal in life: to be happy. Almost everything you do is ultimately related to your search for fulfillment and satisfaction. Maybe you are looking for a new job. Why? You say it is to increase your income. But why do you want to increase your income? You probably want it so you can buy a bigger house, a nicer car, and more expensive vacations. But why do you want those things? So you will be more attractive and marketable to the opposite sex, you say. And why do you wish to become more attractive? So you will find someone who loves you and whom you can love. And, finally, why do you want to love and be loved? So you will be *happy*. Trace your goals far enough and you will ultimately end up in the same place everyone else does. With this in mind, it is important that you recognize that the primary factor that will determine your happiness (or lack of it) more than any other is the depth of intimacy you experience with other people.

A lack of close relationships has been correlated with increased risk of suicide, depression, alcoholism, drug addiction, elevated stress levels, a weakened immune system, high blood pressure, feelings of helplessness, and the inability to sleep. Psychologist John Cacioppo of the University of Chicago conducted a survey of doctors and found that they actually admit to providing better health care to those with a supportive family than to those who are socially isolated. Furthermore, cardiac patients with three or fewer people in their close social network are significantly more likely to die of the condition than those who have more than three. A growing body of evidence suggests that isolation creates a wide range of health problems that may take years or decades to reveal themselves, actually accelerating the aging process. The absence of intimate relationships begins a domino effect of psychological, physical, and emotional difficulties that drain joy from your life.

The level of fulfillment you experience in life will correlate more closely with the quality of your relationships than any other single factor—more than income, more than career success, more than recreation, more even (in most cases) than your physical health. One day in your old age you will reflect back on your life and detect a pattern: your times of greatest fulfillment will have coincided almost perfectly with the richness of your interactions with other people. Happiness is nearly impossible without a network of people with whom you can share your life. Contented people almost always tend to be those who take care to nurture relationships with their spouse, families, relatives, coworkers, neighbors, and other friends. This is very bad news for many people, as society has evolved in such a way as to make the maintenance of relationships more and more difficult. Unlike our parents and grandparents, many of whom lived next door to the same people for decades, the current generation is nomadic, typically living in a home for only three to five years before uprooting the family for a cross-country move. The average American moves about ten times in his or her lifetime. In such and environment, friendships are difficult to build and harder to maintain. Yet cultivating deep and lasting relationships is as important as any other factor to experiencing true fulfillment, better health and even longevity

More intimate relationships result in stronger social support networks, which have been strongly correlated with faster and more complete healing. A study at the University of Texas Medical School in Houston concluded that seriously ill patients with a strong and supportive network of friends and family members were several times more likely to still be alive one year later than those who did not. Other studies reached similar conclusions. People who have a strong social network live longer than those who do not. Strong relationships are associated with a healthier endocrine system and healthier cardiovascular functioning. The heart and blood pressure of those with healthy relationships handle stress better. The immune system's ability to fight off infections is better developed in people with a strong network of friends and loved ones. Conversely, it has been demonstrated that being isolated is as powerful a predictor of poor health as smoking, high blood pressure, or obesity. The fact that deep relationships correlate with longevity may not bode well for many in our culture.

I lived at the end of a cul-de-sac for eight years. During that time, I had only two or three conversations with the next-door neighbors to my right, almost none at all with the single lady who lived to the left. The house just beyond hers was occupied, I was told, by a family of four but *I never laid eyes on them in those eight years!* Their big car would come down the street, tinted windows concealing the occupants. The garage door would magically open, the car would disappear into it as the doors closed behind the vehicle, and lights inside the home would come on. But I never saw those people, save a glimpse of a man riding his bicycle out of the driveway once. A kind elderly couple lived beyond them whom I knew casually. In suburban environments like those a majority of Americans now occupy, relationships don't just happen. They must be sought out and nurtured. This is especially difficult for adult men.

Most young boys have best friends. As they develop from toddlers into young men they generally have a series of best friends with whom they share their darkest secrets and innermost thoughts and fears. But after age 22, the typical American man lives the remainder of his life without a single person he can truly call his best friend. The nature of the male ego demands that a man appear to be more successful and important than he really is, rendering genuine intimacy with any person a dangerous gamble of being revealed as a fraud. Rather than risking exposure as a mere mortal, the typical man opts for loneliness and lives a solitary existence keeping important secrets from his wife, friends, and coworkers. If there is a man he calls his best friend, they rarely speak about anything of a personal nature, staying with safer topics like sports and home repair. Believing he is preserving his own happiness by maintaining an admirable façade, the man actually pushes his fulfillment farther away, as far away as he holds his closest companions.

Those who choose to maintain a public persona that exceeds their private reality tend to avoid intimacy through *pretense*. Like the Wizard of Oz, who feared that his country charm was inadequate for ruling a city and therefore covered it over with the appearance of greatness, they sometimes go to great lengths to create the illusion of wealth, success, and power. Hiding alone and friendless behind a curtain, frantically pulling levers and turning cranks, the wizard posed as one who was powerful and mighty, the exact opposite of inadequate or weak. Certainly, such a man might reason, "Others will respect and fear and envy me. Women will long to be with me, even if only from afar. I'll never actually be close to those whom I presume must admire me, nor will I ever touch any of the women I imagine must want me, but just knowing that I am desired and respected will make me happier." Yet the converse is actually true. The strategy of isolation and pretense never works for very long. More often, it makes problems worse; it reduces happiness. The cost of wearing a mask is high and the price is generally paid in the currency of exhaustion and loneliness. We'll explore this further in Chapter VIII: An Attitude of Authenticity.

I spent several years as the minister of a large church, and had the painful opportunity to listen to men and women in hospital rooms as they looked back on a life that was apparently coming to an end. Some wanted to confess their shortcomings, while others wanted me to pray for them. Others wanted spiritual counsel and guidance. Still others wanted me to promise to comfort and help their grieving families in the difficult months ahead. As I now reflect back on the bedside conversations I had with those men and women, I cannot help but note how few of them spoke about careers and bank accounts. In all those years as a pastor, I never heard a dying man or woman say, "I should have spent more time at the office." On the contrary, almost all of them spoke about key relationships that were seldom nurtured. One man said, "I wish I had been a better father to my kids." Others remarked that they should have been better husbands or wives, more attentive sons or daughters to their own aging parents. Still others wished they had spent more time with their closest friends.

I will never forget a member of my congregation whom I will call Bob. I met Bob when I was 29, just before I founded the church I would pastor for the next seven years. I had the privilege of influencing his life spiritually, and of baptizing him as a 27-year-old adult. He became one of the founding members of my church. A couple of years before, I had met a wonderful young woman we will call Sue. I baptized her as an adult and welcomed her, too, as a founding member of my church. Bob and Sue fell in love, and I had the joy of performing their wedding ceremony. He was the head usher at one of our Sunday morning services, while she sang in the choir. This beautiful love story was suddenly interrupted a couple of years later on a Saturday morning when Bob called me at home to tell me that he had been diagnosed with cancer. Over the next 16 months, friends and family watched helplessly as this robust, joyful man withered away and died. The last conversation I ever had with Bob took place in his modest apartment a short while before his death. He invited me and my wife to come visit him and Sue in their home. Bob had lost a lot of weight, and his hair had thinned terribly as a side-effect of chemotherapy. We chatted in the living room, making uncomfortable small talk as we awkwardly avoided the "elephant in the room" subjects of cancer and possibly looming death. He and Sue held hands until she excused herself to go into the kitchen to fill water glasses for the four of us.

When she turned the corner, out of earshot from us, the direction of the conversation changed abruptly. Bob looked me in the eye and said, "Billy, take care of Sue." Sensing immediately what he meant, I replied, "I will. I'll call her every day." Then he said, "And take care of Mom, because Dad died 10 years ago and now she and my sister will be all alone." I assured him that we would surround his mother and sister with love. He mentioned that all of his coworkers had donated one week of their vacation time to him so that he could be paid during the months that he struggled with his illness. I find it interesting that Bob's last words to me had nothing to do with his unmet career objectives or financial goals. They were all about people.

It should never be far from our minds that by this time next week any of us could be dead and buried. Though I'm making plans for outings or projects next weekend, my family and friends could be attending my funeral that day. A car wreck, an unexpected cardiac event, or a violent crime could abruptly cut my life short. All of the relatives would fly in from around the country, attend the wake, sit through the service, and stand at the graveside. Afterwards, all would go to my house, eat cold fried chicken and macaroni salad, and talk in soft tones. Their melancholy conversations would primarily be about me, as they lamented the loss of a treasured relationship, or as they regretted their inability to penetrate my protective armor to establish one.

There is no relationship so central and foundational to happiness as the marriage bond. If you are married, real happiness will be almost impossible to find apart from true emotional intimacy with your husband or wife. For this reason, long courtships are an essential insurance policy against frustration, loneliness, and emptiness. Great care must be taken to ensure that your prospective life partner is willing to pay the price for true intimacy. It is best if all public masks have been shed long before a wedding ceremony is planned, for once vows have been uttered, possessions jointly owned, and children birthed the process of developing intimacy—or, worse, realizing that it is not possible with the one you married—becomes all the more frustrating. Even a successful career and financial independence are insufficient to overcome the saddening and maddening reality of a sham marriage, one that exists only because the cost of separating appears greater than the pain of remaining together.

For those who are already in such a marriage, bound together by the thin thread of children, mutual possessions, financial necessity, or convenience, there is hope: an intense and never-ending effort to establish intimacy with your spouse. Spare no expense in receiving the best marriage counseling available. Set aside time daily to sit and listen to your spouse. Join your husband or wife occasionally to sit patiently through their favorite television program, rather than retiring to a separate room to see yours. Romance your husband or wife as you did initially, vowing to win back the love of your spouse every day for the rest of your life. Be tender, attentive, and caring. Place your marriage in the intensive care ward and nurture it painstakingly back to health. Be relentless in your efforts to do so. In this way, even the hardest of hearts can be penetrated by the steady drip of years of kindness. Most importantly, begin today.

Chapter VI

AN ATTITUDE
OF PROACTIVITY

One of the most striking differences between success-ful people and unsuccessful ones is their approach to life. Those who succeed are almost invariably those who take a proactive stance toward the future. They do not passively wait for circumstances to turn in their favor, or for someone else to pluck them from obscurity or failure and put them on the fast track to success. Instead, they vigorously work to force circumstances to bend to their advantage. They actively seek out the people who can improve their lives. They create their own "luck" through hard work and perse-verance. They do not "let it happen;" they *make* it happen. Few and far between are the people who succeed by merely reacting to events and waiting for the right opportunities to arise. Fewer still are the Forrest Gumps of the world who are randomly and obliviously blown by the winds of fate into wealth, success, and happiness. While reacting to the unexpected realities of life quickly and decisively is an important skill that all should master, living your whole life that way is a recipe for mediocrity or worse. Proactivity is an essential ingredient of success.

The captain of a ship, if he's a good one, is proactive. In fact, let's create a hypothetical helmsman and call him "Captain Proactive." Captain P. knows his intended destination before leaving port and plots a specific course to get there on schedule. He does not merely hope to get there. He will take his ship there intentionally. He will impose his will on the ship and her crew. Of course, weather factors and currents may force Captain P. to modify his plan or even delay his arrival. He might be compelled to detour around a storm, or avoid an oncoming vessel. At times, the ship would be sped on her journey by a favorable current; at others, it would be slowed by strong headwinds. Engine trouble might cause the ship to lose speed. Rudder problems might cause the boat to veer off course, or even dock somewhere unexpectedly to make repairs. But barring catastrophe, the ship's ultimate destination never changes. The only variables are:

1) when the ship will arrive and

2) the exact course that it will take to get there.

The ship's arrival at the intended port is a foregone conclusion, because the captain is a proactive person. Most people don't live like Captain Proactive, though.

Imagine now a ship captained by a person who is reactive, not proactive. Captain Reactive would, whenever he felt like it, unmoor the ship from its dock and drift out to sea. He would have no idea where he might be going, let alone a viable plan to get there. Once at sea, Captain R. sometimes dreams of lounging on the beaches of Tahiti, but he also has nightmares of running aground on a reef. He really has no idea where his journey will eventually take him. His "goal" is merely to remain employed and pay his bills until he dies. He wakes up each morning and assesses his current location and conditions. Then, and only then, does he decide how he will respond to them. Some mornings he crawls out of bed to discover that the current has carried him overnight in the direction of the South Pacific, and his spirits soar. "Perhaps, at long last, the gods have smiled on me," he thinks. He can almost taste the coconut drinks and feel the warm sand between his toes and this makes Captain R. very happy. He fantasizes about dark-eyed women and palm trees and hammocks swayed by cool breezes and fresh seafood that melts in the mouth. But as quickly as his hopes are aroused, they are dashed to pieces. A storm arises and blows him in a completely different direction. He is now headed for open sea and uncharted waters. He fears his life may become a shipwreck. He envies those who made it safely to the shores of French Polynesia. Why had they been so lucky while he had not? Bitterness takes root in Captain R.'s heart.

In truth, Captain P. is probably no luckier than Captain R. He might even be a little less fortunate, because lucky breaks are completely random and have a way of distributing themselves only relatively evenly over the population during the course of an eighty-year lifespan. But because Captain P. made wise decisions all along, he is better prepared to take advantage of the breaks when they arise. He already has his course plotted, his boat readied with rations and fuel, his crew trained and equipped, and his sails unfurled when the winds turn his way, and he is greatly aided by them. He has lived by the motto of Abraham Lincoln: "I will work and prepare myself, and perhaps my chance will come." Captain R., on the other hand, is caught completely flatfooted by the favorable alignment of circumstances, and by the time he engages his resources the moment of opportunity has passed. Several times in his life Lady Luck opened a window through which he could glimpse the destination he had always longed for, but each time she rebuffed him for his lack of readiness or his hesitancy to seize the moment. Captain R. is not unlucky. His apparent misfortune is due to his slowness to capitalize on the breaks that came his way.

Captain P. is a captain because that was his goal from the start. He became interested in the sea as a young man and decided that he would devote his life to it. As a teenager he enlisted in the Navy to get his training. He worked hard, followed orders, and observed his superior officers carefully, taking notes on everything that happened onboard. With each turn of events he envisioned what he might do in similar circumstances. He rose through the ranks and eventually took his rightful place at the helm. Captain R., on the other hand, is a captain because when he finished his schooling he had no plans. A friend was working aboard a fishing boat and invited him to work as a deckhand while he figured out what he really wanted to do with his life. And he did, indeed, figure it out. He wanted to be a restaurateur. He wanted to open a little café and serve breakfast, lunch, and dinner on Main Street to the people of his hometown. "One day," he thought, "I'll quit this job on the boat. I'll leave the sea life behind and do what I was really meant to do: open a restaurant." On quiet nights aboard the boat, he sips beer with his comrades and talks of his dream to settle into his role as "Chief Cook and Bottle Washer" at his own little eatery. And yet, year after year he continues to work aboard the boat, putting in time, climbing a ladder whose top rung is nowhere near where he wants to be, earning seniority at a job for which he has no particular interest or passion. Twenty years later, as other sailors have come and gone, he has risen to the top rank on his boat by default. He lives his life in regret, only dreaming of a life that could have been. But Captain R. could become Captain P. by following four easy steps.

I. DECIDE ON YOUR DESTINATION

It is impossible to be proactive unless you know what your end goal is. While it is certainly true that all of us, including both Captain P. and Captain R., constantly react to events and circumstances, the proactive person's response is determined by his or her ultimate goal. The reactive among us, on the other hand, respond in knee-jerk fashion to every predicament or happenstance that arises, having only a short-term solution in mind. The proactive person responds (or chooses not to respond) to those same circumstances based solely on the intended long-term destination. A reactive person runs around frenetically putting out fires as they arise, because his "goal" is simply to remain employed or to survive another disaster-free week. Captain P., in contrast, designs a strategy to prevent the fires from occurring as often. His plan includes educating the public about careless activities that cause fires to begin, lobbying for laws that curtail dangerous activities, training and organizing firefighters, and purchasing better equipment for them and devising a plan to spot fires earlier so they can be extinguished before they get out of control. The proactive man or woman has a completely different mindset, and therefore a different—and more desirable—destiny.

The first all-important step on the transformational journey from reactive living to a more proactive approach is setting your goals. At the end of this section, you should stop reading this book and write down specific goals for this week, this month, this year, this decade, and for the rest of your life. Begin with your most long-term aspirations, because the others will all grow from your life goals. What do you want to accomplish before you die? As Stephen R. Covey so memorably details in *The 7 Habits of Highly Effective People*, you must "begin with the end in mind." For example, if your life goal is to become a millionaire, you must then orient your shorter-range goals around that objective. You must determine what must be done this year, this month, this week, and today to move you in the direction of your goal. As circumstances arise, you must then make your decisions based on the desired long-term outcome, not short-term convenience.

A. Goals Must Be Specific.

The most common mistake people make when writing out their goals is to make them too broad. When a goal is unspecific, the path to it is necessarily unclear. For example, if your vacation plan is "to go to California," there are hundreds of routes that will take you there, but you might arrive in a town you don't care to visit. The myriad of possible paths might cause you to become overwhelmed with the enormity of choosing just one of them. After all, pros and cons of each possible route and destination must be weighed and evaluated; with thousands upon thousands of options, the complexity of the task becomes paralyzing. After all, a trip to Yosemite National Park is quite different from the beaches of San Diego, the glitter of Hollywood, the majesty of the giant redwoods, or the hills of San Francisco. Narrowing your goal to "Visit Los Angeles" would make the task less complex, but still quite expansive; there is the Walk of Fame, Venice Beach, Griffith Observatory, etc. However, if your goal is to "go to Disneyland," the decision-making process will be much simpler and the destination is sure to make everyone in the family happy. Similarly, if your goal is "to get rich," rather than, "to own ten profitable donut shops within 15 years," the destination will be so ambiguous as to provide you with little help in mapping a course to get there. When the target is too broad, your responses will become complicated, imprecise, and ineffective. You must insist on shooting bullets instead of buckshot if you hope to make efficient progress toward your dreams.

At the age of 18, I began writing down specific goals for my life. More than three decades later, I still carry them with me almost everywhere I go. Some of those original goals have been removed from the list; they no longer interest me. Many more have been added through the years. As I write this there are 162 of them, more than half of which have already been achieved. It is the existence of *specific written* objectives, reviewed from time to time, that gives my life direction. I find it a very helpful habit to take a few minutes every Sunday evening to write down my goals for the upcoming week. Near the end of each month, I record my objectives for the following month. Similarly, at the end of each year I write down what I'd like to accomplish in the next 12 months. The concrete nature of these specific, written targets energizes me and focuses my efforts.

B. Goals Must Be Measurable.

Each goal must be measurable and objective, allowing you to know for certain whether or not a goal has been reached. "Have a secure retirement" is too obscure to qualify as a goal; it is merely a hope or a wish. "Retire with $3,000,000 in assets" is measurable. You will easily be able to ascertain whether that goal is reached or not. "To be a good parent" is even vaguer. A tighter goal would be, "To see all my kids graduate from college with at least a 3.0 GPA." By defining the completion of the goal in a very concrete way, you may also more easily determine whether you are on schedule to achieve it in your lifetime, or by a particular deadline. If your goal is to retire with $3,000,000 at age 65, you can then extrapolate backwards to determine how much you should save by ages 30, 40, 50 and 60 in order to reach that plateau. The more narrowly you define your objectives, the clearer the path to them becomes. When establishing goals, ambiguity is your enemy.

C. Goals Must Be Acceptable.

If you are married or have children or a business partner, your goals must be thoroughly vetted with those who might be affected by them, especially those you hope will help you achieve them. For example, if your goal is to run a horse farm, but your spouse hates animals and wants to live in a downtown apartment building, the achievement of your dream will be made all the more difficult. If your goal is to see every country of the world, but your spouse hates airplanes, then your goal (or your spouse!) will have to be cast aside. If your goal is to expand your business, but your partner is looking to downsize, your goal must be reevaluated or the business must be restructured. Before spending much time, energy, or money on pursuing your intended objective, make sure those around you are committed to helping you, or at least not standing in your way. Ask the key people in your life if they feel good about your goals, and whether they will be supportive as you pursue them. Make sure that your spouse, children, or business partner understands the role (if any) you expect him or her to play in attaining the goal.

D. Goals Must Be Realistic.

Goals should stretch you, but when they are set too high, the result is predictable: you will not only fail, but you will abandon the pursuit of the goal very early on. For example, if your New Year's resolution is to make $1,000,000 this year, but you've never made more than $100,000 a year in the past, you will realize within a few days or weeks that the attainment of your dream is a lost cause, and you will lose your motivation. However, if you set the bar at a lower, but achievable, level, your energy might persist all year. If you just made the $100,000 mark last year, you should set this year's objective at $110,000. Ten percent growth is a challenge, but can be accomplished. The fact that the fulfillment of the goal is within reach, even if only barely so, will tend to galvanize you and inspire you to summon all your resources to reach greater heights.

E. Goals Must Be Time-Sensitive.

A goal that has no completion date attached to it is not a goal at all. It is a pipe-dream; it is wishful thinking. Everyone has dreams of what they hope to become. Successful people turn those dreams into time-defined goals with real deadlines. Even though they are self-imposed, you must rigorously hold to them as though they had been established by a demanding boss who has threatened to fire you for any delays. When a deadline approaches, you must be willing to work all night, if necessary, to meet that deadline. When you were in school, your deadlines were assigned to you by teachers, and the consequences for failing to meet the deadlines were usually well-defined. It was the fear of those consequences that led you to type into the wee hours, spend long hours in the library, or skip meals to complete a project. When your deadlines are self-imposed, you must discipline yourself to artificially induce that same sense of urgency. In summary, the goals you set must be "SMART," an acronym for Specific, Measurable, Acceptable, Realistic and Time-sensitive.

II. PLOT YOUR COURSE

Once a goal (your destination) has been set, you must establish a clear and unambiguous path that you intend to take in order to reach it by your established deadline. Just as a trip to a distant city requires that you map out a travel plan, a goal requires that a strategy be established to accomplish it. If your goal is to drive from Los Angeles to New York City in nine days, you will naturally have to break that trip into daily increments that will help you monitor your progress and make choices along the way. You will not be able to stop for five days in Las Vegas, then take a side trip to the Grand Canyon for two nights of camping; that would put you far behind schedule. The existence of the deadline adds urgency to your trip and prevents you from wasting time and taking detours that might ultimately prove to be your undoing.

The specific plan also serves to transform mere wishful thinking into an actual goal, one that is not only achievable but likely to be fulfilled. A mere dreamer might fantasize about living a life of wealth and luxury; an achiever dreams those same dreams, but determines the amount of money needed for such a life and then begins a weekly savings-and-investment plan to accumulate that amount of cash. The conclusion is simple: no strategy, no accomplishment.

Years ago I developed a maxim to help me achieve this: "Cut it like a chicken; eat it like an elephant." When a chicken is properly cut for frying, it is severed into easily distinguishable parts: a wing, a leg, a breast, a thigh, and so on. Similarly, your dream of wealth, or stardom, or fame, or success must be divided into manageable steps that I call milestones. Milestones are intermediate goals that must be accomplished as a part of the whole. If your objective is to eat an entire chicken, it's probably easiest to first consume the leg, then the wing, etc., rather than to take one bite of each piece, then doing so again and again in a cyclical fashion. For example, once the major objective of wealth (whatever specific amount you choose to define as wealthy) has been established, then milestones must be established. Your first milestone might be to purchase a rental property by a certain date, and lease it a month later. Your second milestone might be to accrue $100,000 in your IRA. If your goal is to become the CEO of your company, intermediate milestones might be supervisor within one year, manager within three years, vice-president in eight years, senior vice-president in 15 years, and CEO by your 20th year. You can then start gnawing away at the most immediate milestone.

Once the "chicken" has been carved into more manageable milestones, you then choose the most basic or urgent one and "eat it like an elephant." There is an old children's riddle that asks, "How do you eat an elephant?" The only-slightly-humorous answer is, "One bite at a time." Each milestone must be broken down into many tiny steps that are "bite-sized," small enough to be done in a few minutes or hours. Those that might require several days can usually be broken down even further into more manageable sizes. Call them "Goal McNuggets," if you like. These become your daily to-do list. Your grandest goals might involve hundreds or even thousands of such steps, but the time you invest in writing them down will pay you back a hundredfold over the years. You now have your road map in hand. Next, you need merely put a few of them on your to-do list each and every day, checking them off as they are achieved. Persist in this manner for a few years and you will progress mightily toward the achievement of your dreams.

III. MEET THE RIGHT PEOPLE

Often overlooked on a personal road map to success is the list of the people you will have to know (and be known by) in order to arrive at your destination. No one achieves significant goals in a vacuum, and you will be no exception. To the contrary, every successful person is standing on the shoulders of those who have gone before: parents, teachers, coaches, mentors, role-models, and co-workers. As you are planning out your path to your goals, you must make sure to list among your milestones the people with whom you will have to build relationships in order to reach your destination. If your goal, for instance, is to be elected to your county's school board, you will need to rub shoulders with and gain the approval and confidence of some of the political bigwigs in your area, as well as prominent citizens, the Superintendent of Schools, a few principals and perhaps some local TV personalities who can help you get publicity.

Once this list is complete, you must craft a careful strategy to meet and associate with these individuals and groups. What social functions do they attend? Can you volunteer to assist on present city council members' election campaigns so that you get their attention and are invited into their spheres of friends and associates? Are they members of any local civic clubs? Are they members of any trade associations? Do they serve on the boards of any non-profits with which you can assist? What health clubs do they frequent? Do their kids play on any sports teams that you can get your own child signed-up for? Are they active in their homeowners' associations? Are there any causes that they are actively involved in supporting? Could you simply write them a letter and request an appointment with them? Or could you write an article about them for a blog or magazine that would require you to interview them? Perhaps they love sailing, or are huge fans of your local school's football program. The list of possibilities is endless. Do not let your fears that these people will see you as gold-diggers or "users" dissuade you; most of them will know immediately what you are trying to do and be impressed, not disgusted. After all, most of them had to do the same thing to arrive where they are. They will see a bit of themselves in you. But make no mistake: you *must* meet these people and become a part of their lives at some level in order to reach your objectives.

IV. GET MOVING

Of course, all of this is mere talk until you actually do something. And you will probably not do much of anything until all of these steps have been put *on paper* and placed where you will see them frequently. Merely making a mental note to become more proactive and goal-oriented will be helpful only for the few days it takes you to forget that you ever read this chapter. To prevent this from happening, you must put the goals in a prominent place where you will read them often. I've carried my long list of life goals with me in my DayTimer® (yes, I still carry a thick paper daily planner with me everywhere I go) for more than 30 years. When I am on a plane or sitting in an airport lounge or stuck in the waiting room at the dentist's office I take them out and review them. But my more immediate list of milestones and weekly goals I keep on my computer. I've placed a shortcut on my desktop called "Goals" and I open it every morning before doing much of anything else. I review them to find out if I'm on schedule. In fact, I had set my weekly goal to finish this very chapter by this evening, and almost quit writing two paragraphs ago. But I saw on my weekly list of goals this morning, "Finish Proactivity chapter" and it pushed me to crank out this last section. The simplest way to make measurable improvement in your life is to write down your goals and place them where you will see them every day.

Now... quit reading this book for a few hours and get out a pen and paper or sit down at your computer. Write out your life goals and prioritize them. Place a deadline on each one. Map out a thorough strategy for accomplishing them. List the milestones that must be achieved on the path to each one, and a date by which each must be completed. Be sure to include on this list of intermediate goals a list of the people whose help you will require along the way. Then make a long to-do list describing every tiny thing that must be done to reach your first and second milestones (a few of the steps for milestone #2 can usually be taken care of while your main focus is on the first). Place several of these items on your activity list for each day of this week, whether you carry a paper calendar, a daily planner, a simple to-do list, or a P.D.A. Finally, *get moving*. Check each one off as you do it, just as I will now go immediately to my goal list and type "DONE" beside "Finish Proactivity chapter" on my own goal list.

Chapter VII

AN ATTITUDE
OF POSITIVITY

Nothing is more important than your attitude. Did I say "nothing?" I'm sorry, I meant to say, "*Absolutely* nothing is more important than your attitude!" Attitude supersedes every other aspect of your life in determining your contentment and success. Nothing is more important. Not your talent, your education, or your upbringing. Not your attire, or social network, or position. Not your work ethic, or looks, or I.Q. Not your personality or motivation. Not wealth or fame. Not even your genes can compensate sufficiently to overcome a negative attitude. Successful and happy people are almost always characterized by their upbeat, positive outlook on life. For some of us, this happy and optimistic disposition comes naturally; but for most of us it must be deliberately cultivated, nurtured, and rigorously maintained. A sour attitude will cast a cloud over all you do, magnifying the pain of life's challenges and dampening the joys of its blessings. In the same way, a *joyful* outlook will make every good thing you experience even better, and diminish your suffering in even the darkest of times.

I. RECOGNIZE THE CONSEQUENCES

A failure to recognize the power of attitude will sentence you to live at a level far below what you could otherwise enjoy. While it is true that you have the privilege of choosing how the circumstances around you affect your attitude, it is equally true that you have *no power whatsoever* to determine the effect your attitude has on your circumstances. Your attitude is always at work, continually affecting the world around you for good or ill, with or without your conscious awareness or participation. Around the clock, every day of your life, a good attitude is slowly making your life better. Similarly, a negative disposition and outlook are constantly at work exerting a downward pull on everything you do and experience. There is nothing mystical or paranormal about this process; quite the contrary, you should expect nothing other than this very natural demonstration of the law of cause and effect.

In 2006, Rhonda Byrne released her mega-bestseller, *The Secret*. While many assumed that it was just another self-help book, this is far from the case. It is highly metaphysical, if not spiritual; it comes painfully close to establishing itself as a religion of sorts. Ms. Byrne promotes "The Law of Attraction," which states emphatically that when you concentrate on what you want earnestly enough, your wishes are sent out from you like a radio transmitter. The universe, she says, then resonates with your longings and is obligated to give you want you desire. This is absurd. The universe is not a radio receiver and has no power to grant wishes. If the Law of Attraction was true, would one of its most vocal adherents, James Arthur Ray, have seen three people die in a sweat lodge during one of his self-help programs? Did that senseless tragedy "resonate" with his deepest desires? In truth, the Law of Attraction merely attempts to transform a completely natural process into something more mystical (and more marketable!). While the book was wildly successful for Ms. Byrne and her publisher, Atria Books, it is utter nonsense. The "Law of Attraction" is actually a misguided attempt to explain a principle that is much more straightforward, natural, and uncomplicated.

Your attitude profoundly affects your life, not because the universe magically responds to your wishes, but for one simple reason: your attitude changes *you*. Your attitude measurably affects what you do, how you do it, and how others react to you, and those three factors make all the difference. They are the "pixie dust" that a positive attitude sprinkles over your actions to make tiny changes today that, parlayed over the duration of years, makes a huge difference in your destiny. Attitude is the closest thing to real magic in this life. Having a positive attitude motivates you to readily say "yes" to extra work at the office while your less upbeat coworkers avoid eye contact with the boss and make excuses. A positive attitude causes you to do your work with a smile and with enthusiasm and, therefore, to produce better results. And a positive attitude causes customers to say nice things about you, request to work specifically with you, and to buy more from you. It causes other people to enjoy your company more and lessens stress around your home. It motivates you to keep trying when those with a poor attitude would give up. And it causes your boss to take note of you and think of you first when raises and promotions are available. Those who struggle most are the ones who allow circumstances to control their attitudes. Those who succeed are the ones who counted on their positive attitude to slowly build better circumstances around them.

In my profession as a motivational speaker, I travel several times each year to Las Vegas to speak at conventions in the many casinos there. In 1999, I was scheduled to speak at a new hotel in Henderson, Nevada, about a thirty-minute drive from the McCarran International Airport and the popular Las Vegas Strip. I always travel with large, heavy trunks in which I transport my books, CDs, DVDs and props, and I could tell the moment the cab driver pulled up to the curb to get me that he had a bad attitude. He took one look at my obviously-heavy luggage and sighed with exasperation. I apologetically explained that I was a speaker with lots of products to sell, and that I would be happy to help him load them in his cab. He was clearly miffed as he waved me off and snapped, "No, I'll get 'em!" He mumbled and grumbled and moaned and groaned as he wrestled the two seventy-pound footlockers (the largest and heaviest most airlines will accept) into the back of his mini-van. I slid into the back seat as he took his place behind the wheel and asked, "Where to?" He craned his neck to peer at me in the rear view mirror. "The new Hyatt Regency at Lake Las Vegas Resort," I replied. The cabby looked immediately deflated and buried his face in his hands. "What's wrong with that?" I asked. "It's so far!" he angrily replied, pointing out that it was a half-hour's drive to Henderson. I was completely taken aback by his response. I had frustrated taxi drivers in the past by requesting trips they deemed way too *short* to be worth their time, but never for a trip that was too far. I said, "Isn't that what a cab driver wants: a good fare?" "Normally, yes," he retorted, "but this is my last run of the day and I was hoping to get home at a decent hour." I offered to take another cab, but he crossly put the car in gear and pulled out into traffic, way too fast for my comfort. He mumbled and grumbled and moaned and groaned all the way to my destination about how his wife would have dinner on the table already, and that she would be angry when he came home late. When we arrived, he opened the trunk remotely and waited for a bellman to remove my heavy luggage. I paid the driver and gave him a truly rotten tip: *one dollar.* My point is this: I suspect that cab driver went straight home and told his wife that he has a bad attitude *because his passengers are lousy tippers!* He obviously had it completely backwards. His passengers are lousy tippers because he has a terrible attitude.

It would be very easy for any of us to say, "The reason I have a bad attitude at work is that my boss doesn't pay me what I'm worth." That might be true. More likely, though, your boss doesn't pay you what you think you're worth because you have a bad attitude! Or, best yet, perhaps it's a little bit of both, the proverbial chicken and egg dilemma. One begets the other in a downward spiral not only at work, but in family and personal matters, as well. For the wise reader, today would be the day to strangle the chicken, or scramble the egg, and make a decision that from today forward life will be faced with a fabulous attitude. Few issues in life are more important than this one.

II. COMPARE YOURSELF TO THE TRULY UNFORTUNATE

The pain experienced by millions in this world is unimaginable to a resident of 21st century America. Pain to an American is a car that breaks down, a boss who is demanding, a home that is slightly smaller than the neighbors', or two kids in college at the same time. *Normal* life for much of the world is no car at all—ever, an unemployment rate near 30%, a shanty that is barely watertight, and not even knowing anyone who has gone to college. Consider the standard of living in Afghanistan or Bangladesh, the absence of basic human rights in China, the constant strife in the heart of Africa, or the staggering tax rates in Europe.

Many years ago on a trip to India I visited the city of Calcutta, a teeming mass of humanity in excess of ten million people, hundreds of thousands of whom are destitute. Outside my hotel a crowd of beggars lingered night and day, some with no legs, others with cleft palates, many with no arms. Dressed in filthy rags, they repeatedly accosted those entering or leaving the Oberoi Grand Hotel with requests for money. Advised by my Indian travel guide not to be seduced by their panhandling, I refused to give them money for the first few days. But then, my heartstrings tugged by their persistence and longing gazes, I devised a test to see if the beggars were truly needy or mere grifters. After dining in the hotel one evening, I wrapped several dinner rolls in a paper napkin, walked a few feet out of the hotel, and opened it in full view. I was instantly besieged by scores of people who fought over the rolls and desperately attempted to cram one into their own mouths before others might snatch it away. Afraid of being stampeded to death, I tossed the remaining rolls in the air and ran back into the hotel where I watched in horror the mini-riot I had caused.

From the third-floor room where I stayed those eight days, I witnessed below me a heart-wrenching spectacle. At any given time, several people were picking through the mound of garbage produced by the hotel. Some were eating directly from the dump, others were gathering tin cans or other garbage that might be sold for a pittance. All day they came, dressed in rags, worn and haggard in appearance. But one fact riveted me: fully ten percent of those combing through the refuse were wearing a big smile and singing a happy tune all the while. They had learned the secret that is so elusive to many of us, that *life is attitude.*

Misery is quite a relative thing. Many people who consider themselves afflicted with a less than adequate life are actually living dream lives by the standards of most, and not simply by the standards of people in centuries past, but by the vast majority of people alive today. A difficult life by American standards is a wonderful existence to most others. Said another way, one man's misery is another man's paradise. The inescapable conclusion is that misery and happiness are created not so much by circumstances, as by the lenses through which circumstances are viewed or the standard against which your present state is measured. Many a pauper has died blissfully happy, while many tycoons have taken their own lives, apparently overwhelmed by the reality that their great possessions brought them so little genuine happiness. When you compare yourselves to the truly less fortunate, maintaining a positive attitude is made easier.

III. CHOOSE THE STUFF YOU'RE MADE OF

When I was a small boy, there was a dead-end street in my neighborhood. It was about forty yards long, and ended at a small stream that the developer was planning to bridge so that he could build more homes on the far side. But in the interim, he used that dead-end to store construction supplies: piles of lumber, bales of shingles, loads of bricks, etc., which made that short stretch of road a virtual Mecca for all of the children of the neighborhood to gather there and play. Upon our arrival at this makeshift playground one day we were met with a curious pile of tar balls. The builder had dumped several piles of sticky tar balls, each ball about the size and shape of a good skipping stone. To an adult, these tar balls were almost certainly the makings of a future road. But to little boys, they were ammo! We crammed our pockets full of tar balls, and hid behind piles of lumber to hurl them at each other. One day, after just such a battle, I returned home oblivious to the fact that my pockets were still filled with tar balls, and they went through the wash. And then they went through the *dryer*. There, in my mother's warm dryer, those little tar balls melted. They not only ruined that entire load of laundry, they literally paved the inside of the dryer! I don't think I'll ever forget how my mother responded: she put me bodily in the dryer with a hammer and a putty knife to scrape the tar out!

It would be easy to assume that the tar balls melted due to the heat produced by the clothes dryer, but this is not the entire story. Suppose, instead of putting tar balls in a dryer and heating them to 140 degrees for one hour, we put some lumps of clay in a kiln and heated them to 2,000 degrees for eight hours. What would happen to them? They would *harden*. Don't ever allow yourself to believe that it is the "heat" applied to you by circumstances, or the economy, or your environment that causes you to melt. Heat cannot do that. The only thing heat can do is reveal your melting point. It can merely expose the stuff of which you are made, which is good news. Because as human beings, we enjoy the high privilege and incontrovertible right to choose our own melting point, to consciously select the stuff of which we are made. We do that every day of our lives, usually many times in a given day, by exercising our inalienable right to choose our attitude.

IV. CHOOSE YOUR VANTAGE POINT

While you cannot always choose what happens to you and around you, you *can* always choose the way you interpret those circumstances. You can carefully select the vantage point from which you view them. Every problem is multifaceted, but it is human nature to focus on the facet that is the darkest and most troublesome. This is natural, because it is the darkest facet that poses the most urgent need, the most immediate threat. But a quick rotation of the problem to view it from another angle suddenly turns it into something that is not altogether bad, and perhaps even beneficial. A gem that is dirty on one surface may be sparkling and brilliant on another. When a challenge is weighing heavily on your mind and spirit, a good exercise is to consciously choose to view the problem in a new light or from a new angle. You might even list the ways in which the current challenge might be of benefit to you. Other people can often be a great help in this regard.

Others can often offer a fresh perspective of your problems because they are already "sitting" in a different location. Your problem is not a direct threat to them (after all, it's *your* problem they're looking at), so their judgment is not clouded by the same intense emotions or the sense of urgency you may have. In a football game, it is quite common to see a quarterback walk off the field and immediately pick up a telephone. Why? To whom is he speaking? He is usually talking with an assistant coach who is up in the press box, watching the game from above. It is this assistant coach, seeing the game from a completely different vantage point, who can offer insight that the player on the field cannot possibly see. Where the quarterback on the field—who is under intense pressure from a furious pass rush—sees an insurmountable problem, the coach in the press box might see a golden opportunity waiting to be seized. The only difference is *perspective*. The great challenge for all of us is to take a few minutes to walk to the "press box of life," become our own coach, and take a long look at our situation from a fresh vantage point.

Perhaps the most important question of life is this: "Is the glass half empty or half full?" The answer is a simple one: it's up to you. You must choose which half will occupy your focus. The way a person chooses to answer that question will determine more than almost any other factor how happy or unhappy a person becomes. Attitude is life's great equalizer. It would be horribly unfair if the determining factor in one's happiness level was his or her DNA. It would be terribly unjust if one's happiness were dictated by a genetic blessing that causes him or her to think like Albert Einstein, jump like Michael Jordan, or sing like Madonna. What happens if you come into this world jumping like Albert Einstein, singing like Michael Jordan, and *thinking* like Madonna? Are you thereby doomed to a miserable life? No, because you still get to answer the great question for yourself: is the glass half full or half empty? Your answer will determine to a huge degree how happy and successful you become. But whichever answer you give most often will tend to become truer and truer.

Your answer to that great question is a predictor of your future, because if you choose to answer by saying, "My glass is half empty," *it will get emptier*. The consequence of a negative attitude is that you will attract bad circumstances and bad people to yourself, and over the course of your life you will drain your glass to the dregs of all the joy you could otherwise have known. People who are upbeat and optimistic don't like to hang around, date, marry, buy from, or hire people who are eternal pessimists; therefore, the glass-half-empty person is further impoverished by the consequences of his negativity. Like a snowball, the consequences of the sourpuss' negative world view grow and steadily drain the glass even more. But the converse is also true. If you choose to answer your question by saying, "My glass is half full," it will get fuller! Other people are attracted by positivity. When you smile and view the future as bright, you become more attractive to your spouse or to potential suitors. You are more likely to be hired. People are more likely to buy from you or to return to your business. Like compound interest, the benefits slowly accrue over a period of years. By virtue of a fabulous attitude you will attract good things and good people to yourself and gradually fill your glass to overflowing with all of the joy that a life can contain.

V. PLAY THE HAND YOU'RE DEALT

Of course, there are those who made wise choices all their lives, perhaps even had terrific attitudes, only to experience some unexpected and undeserved calamity. James Brady, former press secretary to President Ronald Reagan is one. On March 30, 1981, Brady just happened to be standing in the wrong place when John Hinckley, Jr. opened fire on the president. One of those explosive bullets, dubbed "The Devastator" by its manufacturer, penetrated Brady's forehead at his left temple and lived up to its name. As it was designed to do, the bullet exploded on impact into several fragments that literally shredded the press secretary's brain. The injury was so severe that all three networks erroneously reported him dead. Now, thirty years later, Brady is still paralyzed on the left side of his body, suffers short-term memory loss, and slurs his speech. No reasonable person would deny that James Brady is an innocent and undeserving victim. Nevertheless, he has steadfastly denied himself the luxury of wallowing in self-pity.

Brady was interviewed by Barbara Walters several years after the shooting. He described how one stray bullet had taken away his career, his ability to walk, his ability to control his emotions, his ability to speak clearly. Barbara Walters asked him, "Mr. Brady, are you bitter?" His answer is one that should be emblazoned on the frontal lobes of every person who has ever sought to excuse bitterness, passivity, and negativity by claiming victimhood. He smiled with the part of his mouth that still functions, and said, "You gotta play the hand that's dealt you. Sometimes there may be pain in that hand, but you gotta play it, and I've played it."

Coincidentally, it was also in an interview with Barbara Walters that actor Christopher Reeve echoed Brady's sentiments. Reeve was best known for starring as the superhero in *Superman: The Movie* in 1978 and its three sequels. His brilliant career and charmed life were abruptly altered by a near-fatal horseback-riding incident in 1995. The fall left him almost totally paralyzed until his death nine years later. But only a few months after his accident, he appeared on television with Walters from his wheelchair. When asked if he thought he would ever walk again, he famously replied, "Either you do or you don't. You just play the hand you're dealt. Sometimes you get a lot of face cards, sometimes you don't. But I think the game's worthwhile. I really do." In his fourth and final interview with Mrs. Walters in 2003, he said this: "Being physically paralyzed for eight years, I get pretty impatient with people who are able-bodied but are somehow paralyzed for other reasons. You know, all the reasons people don't become what they could become or don't fulfill their potential, and they're walking around able-bodied. I'm going, 'come on, come on, go for it.'"

Again, *you play the hand that's dealt you*. What a beautiful answer! You don't allow circumstances to turn your attitude sour just because someone else was dealt a royal flush while you got stuck with a pair of threes. Instead, you choose to have a positive mental attitude despite the circumstances. You play your pair of threes with all the enthusiasm, determination, and motivation you can muster, and that is the key to a happy life, and often to a successful one, as well.

VI. FAKE IT 'TIL YOU MAKE IT

There are those who resist this message of positivity, not necessarily because they don't believe that attitude is important, but because it feels phony to them. "Don't tell me to walk around with a big plastic smile!" they say. "I'm no Pollyanna! I'm not going to pretend to be happy when things aren't going my way!" they insist. But these people are missing the central point of the attitude principle. That essential tenet is this: demanding a positive outlook from yourself in the face of your struggles will actually tend to make things better. Forcing yourself to smile will actually make you happier. Being happier will make you more attractive. Being attractive will win you more friends, dates, and sales. A recent study at the University of Cardiff in Wales, found that people whose ability to frown had been deliberately inhibited by botox injections actually reported being happier than those who were able to frown freely. Like a feedback loop in a public address system, your smile increases your happiness, which makes your smile more genuine, which in turn makes you even happier in a continuous loop. By forcing yourself to smile—even a little bit—you will make your circumstances better.

Similarly, by forcing yourself to be optimistic in the face of daunting challenges, you will become more productive. If your sales quota this month is extremely high, but you are optimistic that it is reachable, you will tend to work all the harder to reach it. However, if you feel it is unreachable, you'll be more likely to simply become depressed and go to bed. You'll throw in the towel and fall way short. While the person who is optimistic may not, in fact, reach his quota, he will come closer to it than he would have with a negative outlook, and he will make more money. If you believe the person you want to marry will never have you, you will be under-confident and morose, making you less attractive and less likely to get the husband or wife you desire. On the other hand, if you approach that person with a big smile and an air of confidence, you'll be more likely to get the response you want.

Having a great attitude is not phony at all. It is a deliberate choice to focus on and be thankful for the good in your life (the part of the glass that's full) even as you deal with the bad (the part that's empty). Looking at life this way is no phonier than concentrating on the empty part. It is less *natural*, to be sure. It is certainly less common. This is why it is so powerful; the impact your positive outlook has on others would be diminished if everyone wore a big smile all the time. But to the contrary, the subconscious mind tends toward negativity when it is not disciplined by the conscious will. Most people simply succumb to that tendency toward preoccupation with their troubles. But even if positivity is not widespread, it is still no phonier to concentrate on the good than it is to make the bad the center of your attention. Both are equally valid points of view. The glass is, after all, simultaneously half full and half empty. Only one viewpoint, however, is wise and constructive. It is the act of forcing yourself to be positive, upbeat, and optimistic that tends to bend the circumstances of life in your direction.

A man and his three-year-old son were on a plane together. It was the boy's first flight, and he was excited, so excited that he was becoming disruptive to the other passengers. The father devised a strategy to keep his boy occupied. He turned to the back of the in-flight magazine and tore out the fold-out map of the world depicting all of the routes flown by that particular airline. As best he could, he tore it along geographical lines into several pieces, and mixed them up on the boy's tray table. "Put together the puzzle, son," he said. "It's a map of the world." The man hoped the toddler would stay occupied for a few minutes at least. He thumbed through the magazine for a few seconds, then glanced down and was stunned to see that the boy had already perfectly completed the map of the world. Thinking the boy might be a budding genius or a cartographical prodigy, he asked, "Son, how did you put that map of the world together so quickly?"

"It was easy, Daddy," the boy replied. "On the back of that page there was a picture of a man's head. *Once I got my head in the right place, the world came out just fine.*"

Chapter VIII

AN ATTITUDE
OF AUTHENTICITY

Few things will so sap your joy as consistently as behaving in a manner that is inconsistent with who you really are, because the distance between what you believe and what you do will ultimately be measured in depression. There exists in the heart of each person a longing to find and be the "real me" and to know the "real you." Yet, societal pressures frequently demand that the real you be concealed, modified or shoved deep inside, hidden from view in order to conform to external standards and appear more socially acceptable. Those same pressures make it difficult to know other people intimately because they are beset by the same pressures. We constantly feel demands to regulate our thoughts, our feelings and our words to the degree that much of life feels stilted and artificial. This effect is worsened when the charade is maintained even among our closest loved ones. The degree of difference between the mask and our true face, along with the percentage of time it is worn determine its weight on the soul, and the strain of maintaining the façade can extract a terrible toll on the psyche.

Imagine the stress level of an escaped prisoner and drug addict living in a distant city under an assumed identity. Each day, a disguise must be donned and carefully evaluated for thoroughness. Every few days hair must be dyed to cover tell-tale roots and conceal their true color. The Bronx accent must be meticulously hidden and morphed to sound like that of a true Southerner, or *vice versa*. Cover stories must be carefully memorized and rehearsed. Every possible question that a neighbor might conceivably ask must be anticipated so that convincing responses can be prepared in advance. Wardrobes must be altered to blend into the new environment. Scars and tattoos must be carefully covered up. Each time a siren blares in the distance or a police cruiser passes on the street the fugitive breaks out in a cold sweat and considers whether he should sprint down a nearby alley or walk calmly to avert suspicion. Every location he visits must be constantly evaluated for potential escape routes. A fake driver's license and Social Security card must be obtained. "What if the Feds call my boss to ask about the bogus number?" he worries. "Can the person who forged the documents be trusted with my secret?" the escapee wonders as he drifts off to a fitful sleep each night. With every noise he awakens with a jolt, sits up in bed, and strains to listen in the dark for footsteps as his heart pounds within him. A quizzical glance from a stranger or coworker makes him wonder: "Do they suspect something? Is it time to bolt for another city and begin the charade all over again with yet another identity?" Such is the plight of any pretender.

The consternation level of those who habitually wear masks differs only in degree from that of the fugitive criminal. Keeping track of which lies were told to whom and constantly covering one's tracks consumes so much of the conscious mind's activities that the rest of life suffers. Rather than simply being who we are, which is effortless and liberating, we instead siphon energy from other important endeavors and exhaust ourselves acting out a part on a stage, projecting to the world a self that is quite different from reality. A Broadway actress plays a role for a few hours of rehearsal each day and a couple of hours each night. That is her "work." When the play is over, however, she can cast aside the role, leave it at the theater and return to normal life on the streets as herself. But for the pretender, the mask must we worn almost constantly. As Shakespeare wrote, "All the world's a stage." Like a man singing, *A Hundred Bottles of Beer on the Wall*, he quickly tires of the task, but is compelled to trudge on endlessly, his enthusiasm ebbing slightly with each verse. The pretender's entire existence becomes work, a marathon improv act upon which the curtain almost never closes, and fatigue slowly gives way to utter exhaustion even as the act becomes less and less convincing.

The longer the veneer is held in place, the wider the resultant gap between the public persona and the private self grows, ultimately becoming a yawning chasm which threatens to swallow the pretender. Life has become a stage on which the perpetual actor performs a live juggling act, a frenzied performance from which the only respite is sleep or solitude. He sleeps long after daybreak whenever possible, dreading the moment when he must once again don the mask and go back to his "job" as an actor—an actor playing the role of someone who looks exactly like him and shares his name, but has little else in common with him. Predictably, those who wear masks and play never-ending roles long to be alone. Only then does the curtain fall and the spotlight fade. Contact with other people is rarely enjoyable, because in the presence of others great pains must be taken to preserve the public image. Anyone who might get too close must be pushed away for fear that they might accidentally get a peek behind the mask and alert others to the charade. In this way, the perpetual actor becomes a living cuckoo clock, only coming out when the schedule demands, then hiding away again until the next appointment requires him to reemerge. But there in the darkness, away from prying eyes, there is a visceral, if inauthentic, sense of solace and peace.

There, hidden from view, the pretender can peel away the mask and feel the air on his face. There, he can do anything he pleases without regard for scripts or directors or audience expectations. There, he can voice his real opinions, even if only to himself. There, he is free of societal mores and pointless rules and disapproving looks. His sense of liberation is palpable when he is out of view from prying eyes. His public life has become one of carefully concealed pent-up frustration and desperation. But in private, everything is different. In private—and only in private—he is *free*. Little does he know that these brief windows of freedom are destined to send him careening down the road to slavery, for there—where no one is watching—life begins to unravel. Because his life in public has become so devoid of joy and beset by restrictions and regulations and expectations, those few hours outside the spotlight will be used to squeeze in all of the joy and pleasure he is missing in his public life. In so doing, he plants the seeds of his eventual demise.

When he is alone, the Pretender can tune in whatever he pleases on television, view whatever he desires on the Internet, drink whatever he likes from the liquor cabinet or eat whatever he chooses from the refrigerator, and never fear the judgmental scowls of those who know only his public self. He can eat an entire bag of Oreos, or a half-gallon of ice cream, or both. If he chooses, he can don a hat and dark sunglasses and travel to a casino or brothel where no one knows him. He can give his drug dealer a call and arrange a clandestine meeting. He can call a fellow-Pretender and meet her for a secret tryst. And every time he exercises his apparent freedom, the gap between the man he is and the man he appears to be widens. What began as a crack in the earth is broadening into a gaping canyon, and with each passing week the task of straddling it becomes more difficult. The day will inevitably arrive when doing so is no longer possible, and then the collapse must come.

As the chasm widens the Pretender's isolation must, of necessity, increase with it. Every passing month brings him closer to outright addiction, requiring an ever increasing investment of his resources to satisfy his cravings, anesthetize himself to his pain and recover from his binges. Even if his secret remains hidden, the rest of his life begins to suffer. The time and energy expended by the private self in his veiled activities must be chiseled from somewhere else. He spends less time on his marriage, his family, and his job. Or, he burns the candle at both ends, playing his role during the day while pursuing his addictions as a nocturnal creature. But even this is only a short-term fix, because the lack of sleep will eventually expend all the energy he requires to maintain the public act. In the long run, the end is predictable.

This beginning of the end almost invariably comes in the form of public exposure. An arrest, the noisy departure of a spouse, an abrupt termination from work or a trip to a rehab clinic will thrust the spotlight where it was never supposed to be: on the private reality. At that point, the Pretender is forced to choose: will he be the man he actually is or the man he has played onstage? Or—and there is this third option—will he begin the long and arduous task of reforming the man he actually is, gradually becoming the man he ought to be, the highest expression of who he is as a human being? Will he then experience that grand 24-hour-a-day sense of relief that is only known by those who are *authentic*?

The road to authenticity is simultaneously both painful and delightful. Removing the mask is threatening, yet liberating. There is, of course, the risk that those who knew only the public façade will be shocked by the "new" reality and withdraw their friendship. They might even fire or divorce you, but those people and spouses and coworkers will generally be replaced by friends who will happily relate to the real you. Like the Wizard of Oz, who preferred to be seen as "great and powerful," being exposed as a mere mortal actually resulted in a new and better reality. Freed from the burden of the curtain and the illusion of omnipotence it provided, he is portrayed as charming, winsome and inviting. People don masks in order to gain an advantage, that is, to be more respected, attractive, appealing, or employable. However, the weight of the mask always outweighs the benefits accrued. Eventually, the mask morphs into a burden to be borne, not an asset to be enjoyed. For this reason, one must think long and hard before donning the costume at all.

THE ADVANTAGES OF YOUTH

The easiest path to authenticity may be enjoyed only by the young, for they have the enviable once-in-a-lifetime opportunity to start down the correct path from the very beginning. Anticipating the unavoidable pain the mask brings to all who wear it, the young person may simply choose the better path. He or she can opt to tell the truth, expressing freely his or her hopes, fears, doubts, interests, and desires, while largely disregarding their societal implications. Of course, if those predilections and ambitions are illegal, then all bets are off. In that case, one might be better served to choose the path of secrecy knowing that the weight of the mask, though heavy, would be far surpassed by the trauma of a prison sentence. However, assuming that your goals leave you safely within the confines of the law, honesty is still the best policy.

From the annals of the nineteenth-century British Army there is the remarkable story of Dr. James Barry. He earned his M.D. at only 17 years of age and enlisted in the armed forces, quickly ascending through the ranks to become assistant surgeon, Surgeon Major, then Deputy Inspector General and, finally, Inspector General. On July 25, 1865 he passed away and only in death did he reveal the secret he had carried through more than a half-century of dedicated service to his country and to humanity. It was a secret never remotely suspected by any of his coworkers or the aide who served him for many years. "He" was a woman! Needless to say, Dr. Barry's secret would have required an enormous amount of effort to hold other people at arm's length and resulted in a lonely existence. The maintenance of a veneer necessitates that no one be allowed to scratch beneath the surface.

As a young woman, "James" Barry made a decision to appear to be something she was not and, despite outward career successes, thereby sentenced herself to carry a huge personal burden she could never share with anyone else. No one will ever know the inner turmoil she must have suffered, and the lengths to which she was forced to go to hide her secret. Obviously, marriage was out of the question; no one could be allowed in her bedroom. Contact with family members who knew her as a girl would have to be carefully managed or cut off altogether. Those who knew the truth had to be forever kept away from those who didn't. Public restrooms and locker rooms would have carried their own complications. Her human (and particularly female) need for emotional intimacy would never be met; at best she could enjoy only the illusion of it. Perhaps she initially assumed that her charade would only last for a few months before she moved to a new town and a new job and resumed her true identity. Maybe she fantasized about showing up at the hospital in a dress and blowing her coworkers' minds with the truth. But choices create inertia, and take on a life and power of their own. Like a gauze bandage over a bloody wound, with time masks become increasingly more painful to tear away.

The longer one's mask is in place, the more traumatic the removal of it will be. With each passing year, the mask-wearer becomes more firmly and inextricably bound up with the people and institutions which approve and applaud the values that are only insincerely espoused by the Pretender. As time passes, his seniority in those organizations or societies increases. He finds himself pressured into accepting leadership roles—even if merely unofficial ones—in the groups that genuinely champion the causes and beliefs that he secretly doubts or rejects. He openly gives lip service to those ideals and values while privately wishing he could be with those who hold *his* values. As he publicly "toes the party line" he inwardly feels a growing sense of guilt and dissatisfaction that will eventually morph into resentment and depression. Far better it is to reject that path from one's youth, choosing the trail of congruity and faithfulness to one's true self and ideals. More than four centuries before the birth of Christ, Socrates said, "Better that the mass of mankind should disagree with me and contradict me than that I, a single individual, should be out of harmony with myself and contradict myself." Learning this lesson as a young man or woman is one of life's greatest blessings.

TELL THE TRUTH ALL ALONG, EVEN AS IT CHANGES

Only rarely do people deliberately choose (as Dr. Barry did) to behave one way while being or believing in something radically different. A far more common scenario involves being raised to believe in a certain religion or political system or act in a particular way and only gradually becoming persuaded that this inherited belief system is false, or at least inharmonious with your personal values or viewpoint. In such a case, there is no conscious decision to wear a mask. On the contrary, the person's public persona and private reality are initially identical. However, as doubts arise and are not voiced, slowly the two diverge from one another. At first, the difference between the two is so tiny as to be indiscernible. But gradually the inner person crumbles and changes, leaving the outer appearance apparently unchanged. What was once a true face has been degraded into a mere shell. As in *Invasion of the Body Snatchers,* the person looks and sounds exactly the same as before and carries out much the same daily routine, only with strange inconsistencies. The unsuspecting family members of the newly zombified person notice minor differences in behavior, and worry that something is amiss, but can't quite put their finger on what has changed. Only much later do they realize that the person within has been replaced by someone very different. While the appearance is essentially the same, this is merely camouflage; the thoughts, values and morals of the inner person have altered dramatically. In public, the person's behavior is much the same as it has always been. He travels in the same circles, still shows up for his Saturday-morning softball games and lunches with the same coworkers. But in secret, who knows what this alien-in-disguise may be doing? Calling the home planet? Cavorting with other closeted extraterrestrials? Plotting the overthrow of the planet? The person is no longer truly at home even when he is physically at home. He has been "alienated." Pun intended.

This process of "alienation" is one almost all can relate to, for no one believes as an adult exactly as they did in their formative years. Idealistic college students who protested fervently for liberal causes grow into forty-year-olds with families and mortgages and a conservative approach to life. Black-and-white issues tend to morph into gray as more information is gathered and sifted. Certainties about religious dogmas tend to give way to doubts as reality fails to match expectations. The straight-laced religious teenager rejects those mores and enters a midlife crisis in which anything goes. Or, the opposite may happen: the wild, rebellious teenager might reform his ways and settle into a pew at church. As these inevitable changes and adjustments begin to take place in the mind, a choice arises. The doubts and questions can be openly acknowledged and voiced or they can be hidden. In the latter case, a mask is formed, meaning that close relationships with those who still hold the same belief system must be modified. Those people must be fooled into believing no substantive change has taken place. It is far better to voice those doubts as they occur and remain transparent and authentic. But what about those who have already worn the mask for an extended length of time?

AVOID "COSTUME PARTIES"

Any reasonable person knows that there are certain situations in which the pain of wearing the mask, though potentially severe, might still be greatly outweighed by the consequences of removing it. For example, a Muslim who ceases to believe in Allah might be killed for his apostasy should he be so foolish as to admit his change of heart publicly. A woman who strayed in the past might lose her family if she acknowledges the affair, even one that took place years ago. She carries guilt over the rendezvous, but the pain of breaking up her home—and the damage it would cause her children—would be far greater. Or an actor in Hollywood might come to the conclusion that the liberal politics that dominate his profession are untenable, but to announce his newfound conservatism might end his career. In such cases, a middle-of-the-road approach is to be desired over detonating a truth bomb in the name of total honesty. Contrary to the adage, honesty may not *always* be the best policy. Sometimes it is second-best. Simply because something is true does not mean that it must be stated aloud. There are, regrettably, occasions when putting on a mask briefly is clearly the lesser of two evils.

When forced into circumstances such as this, you should strive not to tell an outright lie. It is one thing to avoid revealing private information about yourself. It is another thing entirely to knowingly say something that isn't true. Determining what degree of self-disclosure is warranted in any given situation is your right as a human being. The public has no right to know what you believe and value unless you are running for office or applying for an influential government job. Do not allow yourself to feel guilty over concealing personal information when the intent is not to deceive, but simply to avoid conflict or causing unnecessary suffering. You have the freedom to reveal or conceal whatever you please, using your best judgment to determine whether revealing the evolution that has taken place in your belief system would cause more stress than concealing it. Wearing a mask is less than ideal, but is sometimes unavoidable for those who started down a path they no longer wish to travel. Total authenticity is a goal, but it is for most people an unattainable fantasy, a utopian vision that may be approached but never reached. Yet, the closer you come to it, the more at peace you will be with yourself and your situation.

When possible, it is wise to avoid situations in which you would feel it necessary to live a lie or to say things you do not believe. To use an extreme example, if you were once a member of the Ku Klux Klan, but have now concluded that discrimination is wrong, it would be wise to avoid KKK rallies in which you would be expected to wear a white robe and recite racist slogans. Perhaps you were once a devout Jehovah's Witness, but no longer believe. You might find it unavoidable to attend weekly services to keep the peace in your family. While uncomfortable for you, it might be less painful than renouncing your faith publicly and letting the chips fall where they may. Such a decision would result in being excommunicated, shunned by family and friends, and exiled from the community. Therefore, it is a reasonable decision to sit quietly in the service and say little. However, accepting a leadership role in the church and leading prayers to a god you no longer believe exists would cross the line into outright deception.

The choice to reveal the true you to the world is one that must be made carefully, because it cannot be undone. It is impossible, once a person has "come out of the closet," to go back into it, unless you are willing to sever all of your relationships and make a new start in another place. If the expected consequences of self-revelation are truly grave, as in the examples in the above paragraphs, the mask may be an acceptable burden to bear. After all, martyrs may be admired for their courage, but they're still dead! But in most cases the consequence of disclosing the real you to the world is merely one of a few weeks of discomfort and awkwardness. In such circumstances, one cannot get rid of those masks too quickly, for every day that you continue in your false persona will increase the pain of revelation for you, and the feelings of shock and betrayal among your friends and family.

ANNOUNCE THE TRUTH

Happiness and relief come when your secret is shared and others are forced into making a choice. Eventually, they will either accept you and love you for who you really are or they will withdraw from you. But those family members and friends who choose to do the latter were never (or, at least, have not lately been) really close to *you*, anyway, were they? They were close to the person whose character you played. They loved a caricature of you, not you. They loved a fictional character. They adored the James Bond they saw, but never met Sean Connery or even knew he existed. Once the role has been stripped away, it need never be played again. This very fact constitutes a huge weight that has been removed from the shoulders of the erstwhile pretender. The time, energy, and mental effort that was expended for years to hide the real you may now be directed toward other, more profitable endeavors.

Attempts to repress your true nature frequently result in depression, which in turn can cause psychosomatic illness, low self-esteem, and even suicide attempts. Depression for the Pretender is a cocktail made up of more-or-less equal parts guilt, isolation, and frustration. The shame over living a lie and then telling lies to cover one's tracks amasses layer upon layer of guilt that settle to the bottom of the soul and harden like sedimentary rock. Added to these layers is the remorse felt for the secret behaviors, themselves, if one believes them to be wrong. For a few, the secret behavior in not evil in any way, such as the undercover Christians in China who meet in secret to avoid persecution. There is no guilt in choosing your own religion or lack of it. Nevertheless, the fear of exposure still takes a toll on the psyche that tends toward depression. For most, clandestine behaviors are those that are either morally wrong, damaging to self or others, or at least frowned upon. Cheating on one's spouse, gambling oneself into serious debt, drinking heavily, watching pornography, overeating in secret or taking drugs fall into this category. Even for those who are not addicted, the Twelve Step formula for alcoholics is helpful in the process toward becoming authentic.

Step Four of the procedure is to make "a searching and fearless moral inventory of ourselves." By honestly looking in the mirror and stating in no uncertain terms what we are, making no excuses and offering no justification or defense for our actions, we might finally get a clear picture or whether serious change is called for. A critical part of this procedure is to make a list of all the people you have wronged and recall specifically how your actions caused them to be hurt. Before you announce to the world your true identity, you must decide whether and how you will change. If you have been a habitual drug user, will you come clean, renounce drug use altogether, and enter a rehab clinic, or will you continue your drug use—just in the open—and simply expect others to accept your addiction? If you are a homosexual, will you divorce your spouse and pursue a different lifestyle, or will you restrain your impulses and try to make the marriage work? If you've been drinking in secret, will you become a teetotaler or simply bring your habit into the open for all to see? Once this decision has been made, the final step toward authenticity is possible.

The methods available to you for publicly revealing your true self vary like the stars. There is the all-at-once public proclamation. In March of 1977, heavyweight boxer George Foreman lost a fight to Jimmy Young in Puerto Rico. Back in the locker room, he had a dramatic conversion experience, after which he proclaimed that he was leaving boxing to become a preacher. The transformation was sudden, public, and dramatic, and rocked the boxing world. Similarly (but in the reverse direction) in 1984 a well-known Christian songwriter and preacher, Dan Barker, sent 50 letters to his closest friends, family and coworkers, along with his publisher announcing that he had become an atheist. The proclamation sent shock waves throughout the Christian world, at least in America. Most of his friends abandoned him, along with his still-devout wife. But years later, these relationships had all been replaced by new ones, allowing him to live openly with his newfound belief, or lack of it. The famous playwright, David Mamet, had been a left-wing liberal for his entire life, but rethought his position. He announced his "conversion" to conservatism in a 2008 *Village Voice* article entitled, "Why I Am No Longer a Brain-Dead Liberal." Each of these men stepped out on the proverbial branch and publicly sawed it off. But your announcement need not be as earth-shattering as these.

For most, becoming authentic means privately revealing your true self to those closest to you, asking them for compassion and understanding, and appealing for their help in your quest to become an authentic person. Perhaps a long talk with each of your loved ones over a cup of coffee will be the best setting in which to bring your secrets into the open. You need not broadcast your revelations to the world; just answer questions honestly when they come up. Don't try to hide the truth from others. Spice your conversation with comments that casually reveal your predilections and weaknesses and others will get the message. When no attempt to hide your true nature is made, an enormous load is removed from your psyche, permitting you to become congruent, one whose inner reality and outer reality are the same. To do so is an essential step in becoming a happy, influential and successful person.

Chapter IX

AN ATTITUDE
OF RESPONSIBILITY

Highly successful people naturally assign credit by looking outward, but blame by looking inward. Their habit is
to peer out the window in search of colleagues to praise for
their team's successes, but to gaze intensely in the mirror to
assign responsibility for its failures. Theirs is the exact opposite of the normal human tendency to bask in undeserved
adulation while pointing the finger at others when there is
blame to be cast. The great leaders I have met as I have had
the privilege of speaking at corporate conventions for the
past fifteen years have all embodied this quality. They were
not bombastic, egotistic narcissists bent on establishing their
own greatness. They did not lead merely by the force of their
position, personality, or charisma, but by the worthiness of
their goals and the loftiness of their standards. They were
surprisingly quiet, unassuming, and humble, which is not to

say they were weak. It was simply that their strength lay in relentlessly pursuing a goal without regard for who received the credit, and in publicly assuming responsibility for the team's failure even when blame could rightfully be assigned to others.

Our society has regrettably embraced victimization as a legitimate and acceptable world view. Encouraged by politicians who benefit from having hordes of citizens dependent upon government as their provider and defender, millions have bartered their highest potential for the supposed security of a welfare check. But one need not be poor to play the victimization card. Here are some notable examples of our tendency to view or portray ourselves as helpless victims:

- Washington D.C. Mayor Marion Barry is videotaped smoking crack cocaine with a prostitute, and immediately claims that he is a victim of racism.

- Leonard Tose, former-owner of the Philadelphia Eagles NFL franchise, walks into an Atlantic City casino and loses fourteen million dollars in a single night. Rather than express embarrassment at his foolishness, he instead files suit against the casino for allowing him to drink while gambling.

- A woman spills coffee in her lap and files suit against McDonald's for failing to warn her that the coffee was hot.

- A teenager steals a car from a private parking lot in Framingham, Massachusetts and is later killed when he wrecks the stolen vehicle. His parents then file suit against the parking lot owner for failing to prevent the theft.

- Clarence Thomas and Anita Hill are embroiled in a public hearing with the nation watching. She claims to be a victim of sexual harassment, while he argues that he is the victim of a "high-tech lynching of a black man."

- Lorena Bobbitt mutilates her husband's genitalia and is exonerated because she was a victim of emotional abuse.

- A Philadelphia school teacher is fired after showing up late for work *every single day*. His lawyer files suit against the school district, claiming that the teacher was discriminated against as a handicap victim. His handicap? His lawyer argued that he suffered from "Chronic Lateness Syndrome."

This propensity for making excuses rather than taking personal responsibility has grown like a cancer in the modern psyche.

"I Can't Help It. I Was BORN This Way!"

With the comparatively recent advent of the field of neuroscience has come an unexpected and damaging consequence. Scientists studying human behavior have actually reinforced the victim mentality of our society by promoting the theory that virtually all behavior is the result of genetics. The polar opposite of Locke's *tabula rasa* philosophy, it suggests that all human conduct is, as they like to say, "hard-wired" into the central nervous system. With them, everything is predestined to a degree that would shock even the most hard-line Calvinist theologian. One's morality (or lack thereof), demeanor, ambition (or passivity), confidence (or diffidence), even one's level of happiness are all predetermined at the moment of conception, and are therefore set in concrete. Does it somehow escape them that by their own line of reasoning they were predestined to reach this conclusion irrespective of the evidence supporting or refuting it? Consequently, even to propose the theory is a self-defeating exercise in futility.

"I Can't Help It. I Was RAISED This Way!"

While some who claim victim status blame their DNA, most still prefer the opposite extreme, opting for the more conventional approach and blaming environmental factors such as family, neighborhood, government, and society for their lot in life. Criminals cite their impoverished childhoods, or the early loss of a parent to death, divorce, or desertion. The poor complain about lack of opportunity. Minorities point to their ethnic backgrounds as an insurmountable handicap. Meanwhile, white males have now jumped on the bandwagon complaining that they are the victims of reverse discrimination. These arguments, too, fail because many people of all races and backgrounds succeed in spite of such supposed barriers and handicaps. And others fail though blessed with every advantage. They do so not because of factors beyond their control, but because of their own decisions and attitudes.

YOU'RE IN CONTROL

The mere fact that millions of people blame their environment for their own failures, while millions of others point to their heredity as proof of their helplessness reveals the actual truth: neither is the real culprit. The purpose of this almost-universal blame game is to find an excuse for one's own lack of success or happiness, and to justify giving up on one's dreams. Armed with this justification one can relax instead of working hard, sleep in instead of rising early and live off of others' sweat instead of earning one's own way. Whichever excuse one chooses—environment or heredity—the outcome is the same: no one is responsible for *anything*. Fatalism becomes the ruling philosophy of the day, and success and failure are viewed as the result of pure, dumb luck. Consequently, the successful are deemed "arrogant" and "insensitive" unless they attribute their good fortune to nothing more than the outcome of a random set of fortunate circumstances. Those who fail are viewed as the oppressed, downtrodden, or less-fortunate.

Whether due to genetic programming or environmental factors, millions of people view—and therefore live—their lives as though they were like locomotives, helplessly bound to follow a set of railroad tracks to a predetermined end. Feeling like feathers blown helplessly about by the fickle winds of circumstance, they assume that God, fate, or happenstance has predestined them to a life of mediocrity or worse, and there is therefore nothing that can be consciously done to change the outcome. One must hope against hope for a "big break:" the appearance of a Publisher's Clearing House van in the driveway bearing an oversized check, the lucky arrangement of numbers on a sequence of ping-pong balls, or a random match on the spinning dials of a slot machine. If bad luck has sentenced them to a life of misery and shame, they reason, a spell of good luck is the only antidote.

A victim mentality is inevitably the mother of despair and hopelessness. Few factors could be as de-motivating, even paralyzing, as the sense that one is powerless to improve his or her state in life. Individuals feel that they are the helpless pawns of a boss, a spouse, an unruly child, government, genetic programming, the economy, oppression, and a thousand other factors. Their view that life is fully scripted in advance becomes an excuse for failing to excel. While the feeling of helplessness breeds hopelessness, the awareness of just how much of life is genuinely under our own control is liberating and motivational. The single most important factor in determining the quality of your life is completely and totally determined by you.

LIFE TURNS ON CHOICES

The primary determining factors in the quality of a given person's life are his or her own choices. The story of any given person's life is being written by his own hand, day by day, minute by minute, in the decisions he or she makes. Just as a door swings on its hinges, life turns on choices. The fodder for many a movie plot has been furnished by playing out the importance of a person's decisions, often made on the spur of the moment, yet with monumental implications. There was the choice to marry rather than break-up, the decision to take the job in Phoenix or go to work in the family business, the dilemma over whether to major in business or education, the option to indulge or to restrain ourselves. All of us can recall pivotal moments in our lives when we made decisions, perhaps seemingly insignificant at the time, that shaped a large part of our lives. For better or worse, such critical moments shape lives and destinies, and their impact is almost always far greater than that of surrounding people, events, or circumstances. Each person bears full responsibility for the choices he has made.

The seeds of success or failure, happiness or misery, health or sickness are often sewn early in life in the form of decisions. The critical choices children make to be obedient to their parents or to cave-in to peer pressure often set the tone for a life of general well-being or law-breaking. Decisions to indulge in alcohol or drug abuse or sexual experimentation in the pubescent years may inflict blows to one's physical and mental health whose effects linger throughout life. Choices to discipline oneself and delay personal gratification until a later time frequently separate future successes from those who struggle financially throughout life. It is typical of those who make poor or mediocre choices to cry that they are helpless victims of a spate of bad luck. It is also typical of them to accuse those who made wise decisions of greed and a lack of compassion. These charges are rarely true.

Follow the case of two mythical females through their fictional, though typical - lives. Betty and Bonnie come from similar households, and lived in the same neighborhood as children. Betty is studious, and takes her homework assignments seriously. Bonnie barely gets by, doing as little as she can possibly do and still pass. Both girls are pressured to drink, smoke pot and experiment with mood-altering drugs. Betty refuses, while Bonnie surrenders. Betty attends high school classes diligently, but Bonnie frequently skips class to smoke cigarettes in the woods behind the school. Betty graduates with honors, a year after Bonnie drops out. Betty isn't a genius, but her grades are good enough to get her into a state university, where she applies herself for five long years, working summers and weekends to make ends meet. Meanwhile, Bonnie is working as a waitress until she gets pregnant by her boyfriend, and they choose to marry at the tender age of 18. Six years later, Betty, now a college graduate and an intern at a local software company marries as well, but is careful to delay motherhood another few years. Bonnie by now has three children, and her husband has long since deserted her. She lives with her parents and uses food stamps to buy groceries. Her wages of $17,000 per year are no match for Betty's $50,000 plus perquisites, not to mention her husband's similar income. Betty lives in a nice home in suburbia with her two young children, while Bonnie languishes barely above the poverty line in a mobile home. Three decades later, Betty and her husband finally pay off their mortgage. From this time forward, the money they had been paying toward their mortgage will go into savings. Bonnie, however, is still paying rent on a dilapidated cottage. Betty's home is now worth three times what she paid for it. She sells it and she and her husband move into a smaller place, pay cash for it, and pocket the difference. Bonnie, on the other hand, has accumulated almost nothing over the years. Therefore, Bonnie decides that she has always been a helpless victim of circumstance, and that Betty got all the "breaks" in life. And Bonnie is *wrong*.

Bonnie is living the life of her choosing, which is not to imply that she would choose her current lifestyle if all she had to do was merely wave a magic wand to make a change. To the contrary, she is the product of decades of poor choices. Similarly, almost everyone is living the life of his or her own choosing. While this analysis will seem harsh to some, to the wise it will be liberating. It means that no one is on a set of railroad tracks leading inevitably toward poverty, obesity, divorce, or unhappiness, because the only circumstance that is impossible to improve is the one made even worse by a negative attitude and poor choices. Freedom comes with the rejection of victimization, and the embracing of personal responsibility for one's own state in life.

Everyone is a victim, but not everyone chooses to view himself as one, and in it is that subtle selection of one's vantage point often where we find the difference between success and failure, happiness and bitterness, action or paralysis. It is, to be sure, impossible to go through life without unexpected detours or catastrophes. "Into every life," the adage goes, "a little rain must fall." No one can control everything; but everyone can control *enough*, if he or she chooses wisely. View yourself as a helpless victim, and you will not bother to exercise your soul's strongest muscle: the right and ability to make good choices. You will instead sit idly on your couch, bitterly watching the world pass you by, filled with envy and wishing you could be so lucky. View yourself, on the other hand, as a free moral agent whose every decision makes your life ever-so-slightly better or worse, and you will be empowered to seize control of your destiny by the sheer power of your will.

It is quite easy to overlook the fact that each person chooses his or her own oppressors. None of us has the privilege of avoiding the pain of victimization. We do, however, enjoy the right to choose whether we endure the discomfort which is the consequence of disciplining ourselves, or the sting which invariably results from our unwillingness to do so. Some people pay the price of regular exercise and a bland diet to stay thin. Others pay the price of poor health for the privilege of eating anything they please and living a sedentary life. Some pay the price of entire nights of studying and writing term papers for the opportunity of graduating with honors. Others pay the price of flunking out of school for the opportunity to spend entire nights partying. Some endure the pressure of working eighty hours each week to climb the corporate ladder, and reap the rewards of senior management salaries and benefits. Most choose to pay the price of lower pay in exchange for the benefits of low stress and lots of free time. In this way we are all victims, but the wise choose to be their own victimizers, while the foolish merely reap the unavoidable consequences of their own shortsighted choices.

In reality, all of us are victims of circumstances beyond our control. We all bear scars from childhood. We all enjoyed the benefits and endured the difficulties of our upbringing. We are all subject to the whims of the economy, the acts of evil people, and the decisions of government. But that which is a reality for all of us grows into a damaging world view for some. It undergoes this unfortunate transformation when we allow ourselves to believe that because we cannot control everything, we therefore cannot control *enough* to make a genuine difference in the outcome, that because we cannot alter the past that we cannot seize control of our future, that because we are victims, we are consequently helpless. At the moment we surrender to these false conclusions, we have thereby chosen a destiny that ranks far below what might have been.

In truth, all of us hold in equal measure in the palms of our hands the single greatest purely human power in the universe. It is the ability to face any circumstance of life, no matter how difficult, with a positive attitude and appropriate constructive response. It is the willingness to accept responsibility for our own position in life and to take upon our own shoulders the responsibility to improve it. Even when one—like James Brady or Christopher Reeve—is a *genuine* victim, life can shaped for the better by refusing to behave like one. If those two men endured the reality of victimization, certainly we can thrive by rejecting the illusion of it.

Chapter X

AN ATTITUDE OF OPTIMISM

Happy and successful people are almost always optimists. Optimistic people are marked by their ability to see the good in almost any situation. They view the world as being full of opportunity, adventure, and wonders to be explored. Their cheery disposition makes them welcome almost anywhere, sought out as party guests, dates, and spouses. Pessimism, on the other hand, breeds the same depressing effect that victimization does. It robs you of your determination to take the bull by the horns and build a better future for yourself. A pessimist views the world through cynical eyes, considering optimists to be phonies, or naïve, blithe ignoramuses. They seek out the negative and feed off of it to reinforce their negativity. Life is seen as a dark place where futility abounds and fate rules. The important factor, however, is not whose viewpoint is correct; there is much truth in either position. The critical reality is that one of these vantage points is productive, and the other is debilitating. One thing is certain: whatever a pessimist might become and accomplish, he would have become and accomplished much more with a sanguine attitude, and been happier along the journey. About half of us are genetically and neurologically wired to be pessimists, but the good news is that a host of studies have shown that pessimism may be overcome by disciplining yourself to internalize three beliefs.

Optimism, first of all, is a belief that you have the power to make your life better. As discussed in the previous chapter, fatalism is the enemy of productivity. Pessimism can sometimes be reduced to an inner voice whispering in your ear, "It doesn't matter what you do. Nothing will ever change for the better. All your efforts might even make things worse. So play it safe and do nothing. Better to create the illusion that you're happy and content with your modest lifestyle than to publicly humiliate yourself by flaming-out while trying frantically to succeed. At least then you'll be seen as a level-headed, grounded person who chose not to participate in the shallow rat race rather than a colossal failure, the one who finished last, a wannabe." Optimism, on the other hand, is the voice that shouts, "If I keep trying, eventually I have to succeed. The odds are in my favor. Sure, if I only try once or twice I'm likely to fail. But if I try a hundred times, or a thousand, I'm bound to achieve my goals. Success is a hard day's work closer than it was yesterday, and will be yet a day closer when I go to bed tonight." Success and happiness inch closer when you force yourself to immediately silence the former voice each time you hear it and replace it with the latter.

Secondly, optimism is the belief that unfortunate and harmful circumstances are an aberration. Optimists will, at times, have the blues. But they view their dark mood as merely a passing sensation. They may have trouble with work or finances, but they still see better times ahead. When an optimist spills coffee on the carpet, he says to himself: "The coffee cup must have been slippery. I'm going to be more careful next time to dry the handle." A pessimist, to the contrary, moans: "There I go again. As usual, clumsy me strikes again! I always seem to make a catastrophe out of everything. I guess this is going to be a lousy day." In other words, the pessimist personalizes and globalizes everything that goes wrong. When he encounters a setback he says to himself, "I guess this is my lot in life. I'm just an unlucky person. Disaster seems to follow me everywhere and I guess it always will. The universe is permanently aligned against me." When a tragedy occurs its destructive impact is magnified, not merely piling on the past letdowns, but reinforcing the pessimist's negative view of the world. If you view difficulty as the normal state of your life, it will be almost impossible to see any circumstance short of winning the lottery as a way to succeed. After all, if failure is the norm for you, any fleeting successes must necessarily be overshadowed and outweighed by the far greater number and severity of the disappointments you are destined to experience. Once again, the result is a feeling of hopelessness, and it is accompanied by the constant temptation to remain passive. The pessimist, like the perpetual victim, has sentenced himself to what psychologists call "learned helplessness." An optimist, however, sees unfortunate circumstances as mere flukes.

Finally, an optimist believes that she deserves all of the good things that come her way and that positive circumstances are—and always will be—the norm for her. When something truly wonderful happens to her she says to herself, "I'm such a lucky person! The breaks just always seem to fall my way. Isn't the world a beautiful place?" When pain intrudes, though, she regards it as one of the inevitable little challenges that befall everyone, whether kings or paupers, ones that will be taken in stride and overcome. Furthermore, she assures herself, the little disappointments I experience could not possibly keep pace with all the good things my future holds. Those serendipities that are destined to fall into my lap will more than compensate me for a few unfortunate events. Furthermore, my hard work and best efforts will render those adverse circumstances less potent and frequent, while turbo-charging the intensity and longevity of the helpful ones. A legion of benefits awaits the person who is willing to drive these three beliefs deep into his or her brain.

OPTIMISTS ARE HAPPIER

The optimist is happier than the pessimist. At first glance, this seems obvious, but perhaps not. Consider the pessimist, who always expects the very worst. He is always either proven to be right—when things go bad—or he is pleasantly astonished by the outcome—when they don't. After all, when you expect the worst, you'll never be disappointed. The pessimist is constantly either congratulating himself for being correct (and expecting others to pat him on the back for his prescience), or rejoicing at his unexpected good fortune. By this line of reasoning, the pessimist seems much likelier to find happiness than the optimist. The sanguine personality is in the unenviable position of often being proven wrong when his best-case-scenario fails to materialize, so he is frequently disappointed. On those rare occasions when the dream comes true, it's exactly what he was expecting anyway. Optimists tend to bite off more than they can chew, often ending up with broken dreams. Despite these factors, research has shown over and over again that optimists are happier people.

The opportunity to enjoy greater happiness should cause anyone with a negative outlook to move heaven and earth to exchange a depressing attitude for an optimistic one. The realism of the pessimist is often helpful in preparing for, avoiding, and protecting against, calamity. However, when negative outcomes are routinely expected—not because of the facts on the ground, but because of a gloomy world view—realism has degenerated into something very harmful. In short, pessimists are unhappy because they feel that they have nothing to look forward to. They look to the future and see little more than pain and failure which must inevitably degenerate into poor health and death. To the pessimist, life is bad and destined to get worse. The pessimist is the embodiment of the old joke:

> *A man went to a fortuneteller. She peered into her crystal ball and intoned, "I have good news and bad news. The bad news is that you will experience nothing but pain and misery every day of your life. The good news is... you'll live to be 120!"*

The pessimist always sees the light at the end of the tunnel as a train headed his way. To the optimist, though, life is good and getting better. Despite the fact that all of us must die in the end, the optimist sees death as merely the conclusion of a happy and well-lived life. *Note that the circumstances of the optimist and the pessimist are the same!* The difference is in their outlook. And the person who chooses the optimistic outlook will live the happier life. Optimists will usually be more successful than pessimists, as well.

OPTIMISTS ACHIEVE MORE

Optimists achieve more because they believe they will succeed in spite of any degree of difficulty encountered along the path to a given goal. Pessimists look at challenges as insurmountable obstacles and throw in the towel at the first sign of trouble. For this reason, pessimists rarely set world records, build successful businesses or create groundbreaking organizations. Pessimists look at a difficult challenge and say, "It's impossible" so they never try. Optimists look at the impossible and say, "It's going to take a little longer and a lot more effort" and set to work. Roger Bannister is the classic example of this principle. A century ago, it was almost universally believed that it would be impossible for a human being to run a mile in under four minutes. Doctors wrote books speculating that if a person ran that fast his heart would stop under the strain. But then, on May 6, 1954, Bannister broke that fabled mark. Suddenly, an amazing thing began to happen worldwide. Records started falling everywhere. A paltry three weeks later a fellow Briton named Diane Leathers became the first woman to run a five-minute mile. Three weeks later an Australian named John Landy, running in a track meet in Finland, became the second man to run a four-minute mile, and did if faster than Bannister had done it less than two months earlier. By the end of 1957—just two and a half years later —seventeen men had run a mile in under four minutes. Could a reasonable person believe that so many world-class milers got that much faster in such a brief window of human history? Or does it make more sense to believe that the only thing that had changed was what they believed was possible? I suggest that seventeen men who had previously been pessimistic about the prospects of breaking that supposedly impenetrable mark had suddenly transformed into optimists. And their optimism resulted in greater effort and success.

Researchers from Duke University's Fuqua School of Business surveyed 232 MBA students to determine their level of optimism, their belief that good things would be the norm for them, to see if their outlook affected their future job searches. Even when equipped with identical degrees and skills, optimists fared much better in the job market. They worked less intensely to find a job, but received offers sooner than their pessimistic counterparts. Furthermore, once they landed a job, they were almost 10% more likely to be promoted within the first two years. Optimists, apparently, made a better impression on their interviewers. They were seen as representing a potential addition to the workplace atmosphere instead of a drain upon it. Presumably their winning smile communicated confidence that they could do the job well, and their cheery disposition was viewed as a welcome change to the sometimes-dreary office environment. Other studies reveal that optimists get better performance evaluations, higher pay and have higher sales. In a study of male undergraduates of Harvard University begun in the 1940s, a high level of optimism at age 20 was correlated with higher incomes and greater job satisfaction at 65. Furthermore, a high percentage of the more pessimistic college students could not even be found at age 65, suggesting they had less stable residences and less prestigious careers, or had perhaps even died at a disproportionate rate. There are even more benefits to a positive outlook.

OPTIMISTS HAVE BETTER RELATIONSHIPS

For decades one of the juicier bits of grist for the rumor mill was the statistic that a woman over 40 has a better chance of being blown up by a terrorist than of finding true love with a good man. But this pessimistic viewpoint has been forced to relent to two indisputable facts:

1) Women over 40 look a lot better than they used to, and

2) A lot more people get blown up by terrorists than in days gone by!

There is reason for optimism among those seeking romance, and that reason is… optimism, itself. A positive thinker, all other factors being equal, is simply more attractive than a sourpuss. Almost anyone would rather be friends with, date, or marry someone who is generally upbeat and chipper than a gloomy, defeatist prophet of doom. The smile of the sanguine says, "I like you," and is more likely to evoke a similar response from others. It says, "I'm open to conversation," and conversations are the doorway to friendships and love. Pollyanna would be a much more desirable party guest than Debbie Downer, because spoilsports spoil whatever sport they participate in. Killjoys kill the joy of those around. Party poopers poop all over whatever party they may attend. But merrymakers make things—and relationships—merry. One might conclude that naysayers cause potential friends, dates, and mates to, well, say "nay." Or, at least, "Nay, thank you."

Optimists are more likely to try to look for the best in their loved ones. Unless driven by undeniable facts to the contrary, they give other people the benefit of the doubt. In a 2006 study of dating couples from the *Journal of Personality and Social Psychology*, researchers concluded that optimism often leads to more-satisfied and longer-lasting relationships. During a quarrel, they discovered that an optimist has less desire to attack his or her sweetheart's flaws, but instead seeks to focus on the constructive things the partner says. One week after the argument, both partners were happier and felt the spat had been better resolved than in couples with a more pessimistic bent. The hopeful nature of optimists causes them to see a bright future in a sometimes-difficult courtship, leading them to strive harder to save or improve the relationship. The pessimist, however, is more likely to quickly conclude that the relationship is hopeless and doomed—just as he secretly feared from the start. Now, the cynic is forced to choose between two horrible options. Either the relationship must be painfully severed, leaving the pessimist with presumably no hope of ever finding true love (after all, he's a pessimist, right?), or he can choose to stay in an empty relationship with, he assumes, no hope of significant improvement. Like so many human qualities, pessimism becomes a self-fulfilling prophecy. If you think a relationship is hopeless, your negativity will drain it further. If, on the other hand, you see your troubled relationship as potentially satisfying, your cheery disposition will have an elevating, edifying effect.

OPTIMISTS ARE HEALTHIER

People who view the future with optimism are generally healthier than pessimists. According to an article in *The Archives of General Psychiatry* in November, 2004, optimists have a 55% lower death rate from all causes than their negative counterparts do. The study also linked cardiovascular death with depression, and noted that optimists have a 23%

lower risk of contracting such diseases. The May, 2008 issue of *Harvard Men's Health Watch* investigated the connection between optimism and health. They found that highly pessimistic men were *three times* more likely to develop hypertension and that optimistic coronary bypass patients were only *half* as likely as pessimists to be readmitted to the hospital with complications. Furthermore, pessimistic men were more than *twice* as likely as fervent optimists to develop heart disease. In a study conducted by the Mayo Clinic in Minnesota, the medical histories of 839 people were tracked over 30 years. All had completed a standard personality test between the years 1962 and 1965 for the purpose of measuring their optimism. There were 124 optimists, 197 pessimists and 518 in between. Three decades later their death rates were compared and *every 10-point increase in pessimism was associated with a 19 per cent increase in death rate*! I've italicized the ratios because they are astonishing. Medical studies frequently conclude that people who, for example, drink a glass of wine each day might be 12 percent more likely to develop or avoid a particular disease condition. But the percentages from the Harvard study on optimism vary between 200% and 300%! Such definitive and indisputable results are both rare and shocking. Optimism has also been show to lower stress hormones, reduce inflammation and lower blood pressure. Optimists recover more quickly from surgery, have healthier pregnancies and experience fewer aches and pains. Pessimism, on the other hand, has been linked to suppression of the immune system, Parkinson's disease, dementia and increased deaths from cancer. Even correcting for the natural tendency of healthier people to see their futures more optimistically, the results remained unchanged. These differences are both definitive and staggering in their scope.

Experts suggest that optimists are healthier because they take a more active role in maintaining their health and utilize more constructive coping strategies. It stands to reason that those who believe their golden years will be truly golden would seek to extend their lives as long as possible, while those who envision poverty, obsolescence and poor health might just rather "get it over with" sooner. Pessimists tend to worry incessantly about problems, which often increases stress levels and raises blood pressure, while optimists choose to create strategies to overcome their struggles. As an alternative to throwing in the towel to habits like smoking or excessive drinking, their positive personalities lead them to genuinely believe they can change, that they can reduce or quit their consumption altogether. Instead of viewing themselves as permanently obese, they see changes in diet and lifestyle as achievable and helpful long-term objectives. Rather than harboring resentments and nurturing them for years after a perceived insult or slight, they tend to forget them and move on. Optimism also seems to have indirect physiological benefits. For example, since optimists are more frequently employed, get better jobs and tend to make more money than pessimists, it seems reasonable that they would also be able to afford better health care and use it more often.

There is yet another reason optimists usually enjoy better health. Optimism leads to better relationships, and those relationships, as discussed earlier in this book, correlate with better health and longer lives. The pessimist's gloomy outlook tends to isolate him, leading to poor health, which gives him even further reason to be negative about his future. The optimist's cheerful demeanor, on the other hand, attracts people with whom he can enjoy meaningful relationships, leading to better health, and providing yet another reason to anticipate a bright future. But the optimist's improvement in physical health is matched by his mental health, as well.

As you might expect, people with positive outlooks are healthier emotionally and mentally—not just physically—than are their negative counterparts. A multitude of studies have indicated that pessimists are at greater risk of severe depression, obsessive compulsive disorders, severe anxiety and sleeping problems. Optimists build healthier networks of friends who are likely to support them in a crisis, help them with difficult projects or accompany them to fun places and events. They are more likely to eat nutritionally and have outside interests. The health benefits of sanguinity clearly extend beyond the purely physical realm.

HOW TO CHANGE
FROM PESSIMISM TO OPTIMISM

To be fair, it must be mentioned that pessimism has its benefits. Optimism must not become confused with blind foolhardiness. The majesty of Wall Street has not infrequently been marred by the bloodied bodies of optimists who jumped from buildings when their rosy prognostications failed to materialize. Better to be a pessimist when it comes to crossing a frozen pond, stepping into traffic, or buying a used car! Optimism shouldn't be confused with rashness or irresponsibility. It doesn't mean ignoring facts, warning signs or common sense. It does not mean being glibly bullish when economic factors indicate a bear market. Expecting your own future to be generally bright does not mean that you blithely expect *every* turn of events to fall in your favor; it means believing that however they might fall, you possess the resources to turn those circumstances to your advantage and live a full and happy life either because of or in spite of them. It means being confident that you will ultimately win the game even if you fall behind on the scoreboard temporarily. Your optimism, in and of itself, will cause you to fight harder to even the score and eventually pull ahead. An expectation of defeat, however, will deflate you and become your reason for giving up and merely waiting for the clock to run out so that you can go home and nurse your wounds. The wise approach to life is to prepare for the worst-case scenario, while expecting the best. Plan so that you will be prepared if the weather, or the market, or circumstances go south, while wearing the cheerful smile and nature of the optimist in all that you do.

Pessimism is a bad habit and—like all habits—can be broken with time and discipline. Optimism is a set of coping skills, and these skills may be learned by almost anyone. The most effective strategy in making the transformation from negativism to positivity is to have an internal argument with your pessimistic side whenever it crops up. There are three steps to the process:

1) Identify a pessimistic thought when it arises.

2) Ask yourself if pessimism is warranted and healthy in this particular situation.

3) Correct exaggerated or unwarranted negativism with positive and optimistic thoughts.

Just because a thought is negative does not mean that it is necessarily pessimistic. The belief that it will rain on your outdoor event is pessimistic three weeks out during a drought. It is pessimistic if you expect rain simply because you believe that you are fated by the stars to experience bad luck for your whole miserable existence. It is pessimistic if you turn every setback into a global conspiracy to ruin your whole life. But harboring the same belief the day before the event when the forecast is for an 80% chance of rain and you have observed with your own eyes the storm making its way toward your town on the TV weatherman's radar, is not. In the face of strong evidence, this is realism, which is wise and healthy. Pessimism would mean responding to the confirmed likelihood of rain by concluding that your event will now become a catastrophe regardless of what you do. Optimism would be resolving to prepare properly for the weather so that the event might be a raging success anyway. When you determine that a given thought wandering through your cerebellum is not realism but is instead the dark voice of your inner pessimist, you can and must correct your thinking.

When you realize that your negativity in a given situation is simply a reflection of your tendency to paint the world in drab colors, you should immediately reword the mental message in more realistic terms. If you are slated to give a speech and the voice inside of you screams that you will be humiliated by your incompetence and never be able to show your face in town again, you should recognize this assessment as a gross exaggeration. Instead, you should reword the statement to reflect objective reality. Tell yourself, "I'm certainly not an orator, but I can make some appropriate remarks that will add to the event. I've heard some boring speeches before, but I've never thought of the person who gave it as a colossal failure unworthy of my friendship. I'll probably do fine, and even if I'm no good, no one will remember it in two weeks anyway. On the other hand, if I work really hard I might even do a good job and people will admire me for my comments and poise." The key difference between the optimist and the pessimist is the way they "explain" circumstances to themselves. By disciplining your mind to convert pessimism into realism you will eventually transform your demeanor. In so doing, you will also earn for yourself the multitude of rewards and benefits enjoyed by the optimist.

The power of optimism lay not so much in what it provides for us as in what it compels us to do. It is not a magical power. There is no goddess named Sanguine doling out favors from Mt. Olympus on positive people only. Optimists are not happier because of who they are; they are happier because of how they behave. Optimism is merely a belief that the future is bright and that my actions can make it even brighter. People who hold this belief differ from pessimists in two glaring ways:

1) They do different things and,

2) other people respond to them differently.

Pessimism is the assumption that the future is dark and foreboding and that there is nothing that I can do to significantly improve my destiny. The direct result of harboring this negative belief is that I have little motivation to engage in the behaviors that build a better future, and other people tend to avoid me so as to prevent my negativism from rubbing off on them. Optimism motivates me to engage more fully in preparation for the future, and to seem more pleasant and attractive to potential dates, friends, and employers. Optimism is a choice, and in selecting it I am thereby deciding to improve my fortunes. Put simply, when you expect good things to happen, those good things become even more likely to occur. When you anticipate bad things, your very expectation makes those bad things more probable. The optimist and the pessimist are both usually right, so make sure you're an optimist.

Chapter XI

AN ATTITUDE
OF CONFIDENCE

Self-confidence is the foundation of successful living. Our level of confidence—or lack of it—affects almost everything we do and how we do it. Confidence abounds in the hearts of small children. As tots, we were convinced we could do almost anything. We were certain that one day we would fly to Mars, or be inaugurated as President of the United States, or rule the NBA with earth-shattering dunks. But then, unexpected impacts against the hard rock of reality scratched the polished surface and eventually carved deep scars into that self-assurance. With each mistake, failure, or criticism the furrows grew imperceptibly deeper, eventually replacing boldness with fear, eagerness with hesitancy, poise with uncertainty and doubt. Where once there stood a monolithic, invincible, boundless confidence in ourselves there now exists a mere shell. Perhaps unchanged on the outside, the inner core is now largely void of hope and positive expectations. Grand visions of future accomplishments are replaced with smaller ones. In order to preserve the small shreds of self-respect we still retain, the subconscious mind redefines success as merely growing old and avoiding bankruptcy. The well that once gushed with self-possession and daring now oozes the sludge of insecurity and timidity.

Even a gifted, skilled, and capable person cannot perform optimally without self-confidence. Confident people take the initiative; under-confident people waiver until the opportunity has passed them by. Confident people stick with their dream despite obstacles; the under-confident throw in the towel and never see the results for which they yearn. Confident people approach, meet, and befriend the important people who can help them reach their goals; under-confident people assume the VIP "wouldn't want to waste time on me, anyway." The confident boldly accept new challenges that cause the diffident to flee. Confident singles walk right up to and introduce themselves to the people they find attractive; not-so-confident ones assume the role of wallflower, hoping against hope that the object of their interest will assume the role of initiator, instead. The dauntless have a decided advantage over their unsure counterparts, if only because they push their boundaries and try more things. They are, therefore, mathematically more likely to find success in at least one of them. But there are other reasons the self-assured do better in life and love.

Self-confidence inspires others to believe in you. If you were in need of triple-bypass heart surgery, would you be more likely to choose a surgeon who tells you, "I've done scores of operations like these. Yours is a very straightforward case.

You'll be fine." Or would you pick the doctor who shakes his head and says, "I don't know. This is a really complicated operation. I'm not sure if I'm up to it. But I guess I'll give it a try."? Who are you more likely to date: the person who looks you in the eye or the one who averts his or her eyes while awkwardly pawing the floor with their feet? Who will you choose to hire as your employee; the person who shakes your hand firmly and tells you, "I can do this job" or the person whose body language communicates fear and trepidation? Who would you rather work for: the woman who stands tall and leads from a position of confidence in the company's future, or the one who slumps his shoulders, furrows his brow, shakes his head and says, "I'm not sure we'll be able to make it through the year?" Like so many of the attitudes endorsed in this book, self-confidence works because it changes how you behave and how you are perceived by others. In many cases, those two factors are the difference between success and failure.

Confidence is not hereditary; it is learned. It is either slowly accumulated or eroded over a period of years as small successes build upon one another or as tiny failures snowball into an avalanche of self-doubt and uncertainty. For this reason, goals must be reasonable, or at least broken down into manageable steps. A person who is only five feet tall sets himself up for failure if he establishes a goal to dunk a basketball. However, if he instead establishes a goal to improve his vertical jump by one inch over a six-month period, and strives to do the same over the next half-year, he may one day achieve that dream. If not, he has at least built confidence in his ability to steadily improve. Setting a goal to write a book is a noble objective, but with each passing year your failure to do so will sap your confidence and reinforce the impression that you are incapable of doing so. However, if you set your goal to write an outline for your book, you might complete the task in an hour and in so doing buttress your confidence. Your next goal would then be to write the introduction, then the first page, then to complete a chapter. As the book lengthens, your confidence will increase. As the completion of the book nears, you'll find yourself working harder and longer on it, just as a long-distance runner accelerates to a sprint when he sees the tape at the finish line. It is imperative that each and every large goal you have be broken down into simple steps in this manner.

Confidence also varies from activity to activity. A man who is downright cocky about his ability to hit a golf ball straight down a fairway might become a shrinking violet with regard to his ability to sell insurance. A woman who boasts of her ability to cook a fabulous lasagna might become a shaking leaf when confronted with using a computer. The lower your confidence level is in a given activity, the smaller and more bite-size your initial measure of success must be. While long-term goals for important tasks (ones that are important *to you*, anyway) might be huge, the immediate goals and milestones you set for yourself should be tiny, even incremental. When attempting a large project, especially one that you deem outside your comfort zone, it is helpful to list every minute step that must be accomplished to fulfill it, then put a box next to each one so that you may check it off when it is completed. The steady accumulation of check marks serves to build confidence that still more are to follow, leading progressively to the achievement of the larger objective. Three strategies might help you start aggressively down the road to self-confidence.

I. START SMALL

When you find your confidence and motivation flagging, small successes are very helpful in jump-starting your ambition. I've made it a practice for many years whenever I find myself unmotivated and without much direction to list about a dozen to twenty small projects I've been putting off and do them all in a single day. The list might include simple items like learning a new song on the guitar, repairing the backyard fence, painting the ceiling in the living room, making a needed change to a checking account, researching an interesting topic on the Internet, etc. By starting early in the morning and working diligently to complete each item on the list before bedtime I find my spirit encouraged and my passion returning. Those small successes whet my thirst for more and rekindle my confidence and drive, and prepare me for the second step in squelching my self-doubts.

II. START WITH THE AREAS IN WHICH YOU EXCEL

If you spend most of your time doing things you're not suited for or skilled at, your confidence will likely suffer. While it is important to learn new skills and expand your horizons, it is equally important that you also undergird your confidence with a few activities that bolster your sense of personal competence and garner the respect of others. If you are an excellent pianist, be sure to keep your skills sharp and play in the presence of others from time to time. If you are an exceptional cook, invite others over for dinner. In so doing, you will receive the approbation, compliments, and approval from others that are essential to building self-confidence—the type of confidence that may then spill over to keep you going in tasks that you find difficult or challenging. Then, when you stare demanding duties in the face, you'll have a reservoir of confidence stored up for the task. But even if you don't, there's a third tactic upon which you can rely.

III. PROJECT CONFIDENCE EVEN IF YOU DON'T HAVE IT

Acting confident—even when you're feeling unsure of yourself—can actually lead to increased success and buoy your sense of true confidence. The old saying, "Fake it 'til you make it" is both relevant and helpful. When you discipline yourself to walk with purpose, stand with shoulders erect, and make eye contact with others, you make a positive impression that will generally create positive results. When you force yourself to walk right up to another person, smile, and shake hands firmly, you improve the likelihood that you will be liked. Dressing as though you are enjoying success and expecting more tends to actually beget both. Those who are perceived as confident are naturally followed by others and recruited to positions of influence and leadership. Our society is overwhelmed today with so-called celebrities who have never achieved anything other than becoming famous for their outrageous behavior. Paris Hilton and the Kardashian family possessed enough confidence to thrust themselves into the limelight simply because they felt worthy of adulation. If the principle works for those with little or no talent, self-control, or accomplishment, it will certainly work for those with a strong work ethic and determination.

One of the most renowned pianists of the first half of the 20th century was the elegant, mysterious Olga Samaroff. She was the first pianist from her country to receive a scholarship to the prestigious Paris Conservatoire in France. She would perform with the New York Symphony Orchestra and the Boston Philharmonic in her mid-twenties. Later, her fame would grow as the music critic of the *New York Evening Post.* Her confident bearing and regal manner were typical of the famed Russian musicians of her time; and that name—*Olga Samaroff*—flowed mellifluously off the tongue in a manner befitting a member of the Russian aristocracy. But Olga Samaroff was not an aristocrat. Nor was she even Russian. For Olga Samaroff was really a *Texan,* born a stone's throw from the Alamo in San Antonio. And her real name, believe it or not, was *Lucy Hickenlooper!* Little Lucy Hickenlooper stands today as an excellent example of the simple principle that other people will tend to view you and treat you in a manner that mirrors what you see in yourself. Carry yourself with the posture of a loser, and you will consistently lose, because people will assume that you know yourself better than they do. And who wants to hire, date, marry, befriend, or loan money to a loser? But comport yourself like success, and success will almost certainly follow you! Whatever your attitude—good or bad—it will tend to wrap itself in flesh and become reality within you and around you.

A friend of mine grew up in South Africa, where his grandfather was a corn farmer. One of the great challenges of growing crops in that part of the world is the tiny monkeys who routinely emerge from the forest to forage for food in the fields. Of particular irritation to the farmers was the inefficient manner in which the monkeys would steal the harvest. A single monkey would stand before a stalk, break off two or three ears of corn, and tuck them under its arm. It would then do the same for another stalk, but in the process drop one or two ears on the ground. Moving from stalk to stalk, it could strip an entire row of corn while only carrying off a few ears that it could eat. Dozens more would be left on the ground to rot. Lacking the modern technology we now possess, the farmers of that bygone era were forced to utilize some creative strategies for capturing, dissuading, or preoccupying the creatures. My friend described the procedure he observed.

His grandfather would obtain a gourd, hollow it out, and then bore a hole about the size of a half-dollar in the bulbous end. He would then drive an iron stake deep into the ground between his cornfield and the forest, and use wire to tie the gourd securely to it. Finally, he would fill the gourd with a monkey's favorite treat: sunflower or pumpkin seeds. The trap laid, his grandfather could go about his usual activities. An unsuspecting ape would appear from the forest expecting to eat corn, but quickly locate its favorite snack inside the gourd. He would reach through the hole to retrieve the tasty seeds, but when grasping them his fist was too large to fit back through the opening. The monkey could easily escape by simply letting go of the seeds, but instead would scream, claw, gouge, and even pull its arm out of joint, clinging tenaciously to the prized snack. The farmer, seeing the struggling primate, would meander toward the gourd in no particular hurry. The ape, spying the approaching human, would struggle mightily to extract the delicacy from the gourd. With every step taken by the approaching farmer, the monkey became more frantic. By the time Grandpa arrived at the trap, the ape was hysterical. He would do anything in his power to avoid capture... *except let go of the seeds!* My friend told me that his grandfather would grab the ape by the wrist, jerk its hand out of the gourd and literally punt that money as far into the jungle as possible, hoping he would learn his lesson and never return.

Low self-expectations are much like that handful of seeds. There is great security in clinging to the belief that you are mediocre or worse. The illusion of mediocrity is so alluring that we cling to it with white knuckles, because it provides a ready and convenient excuse for never fulfilling our potential. After all, if you never expect to be a millionaire, an author, a CEO, or a celebrity then failure to achieve those pinnacles is relatively painless. If you live your entire lifetime expecting to die in obscurity, never having excelled at anything then the sting of defeat is avoided or soothed. If you never try out for the team you are guaranteed never to lose, but you are also destined never to win. In setting low goals (or no goals at all) you are insulated from the potential pain and embarrassment of falling short of them. In clinging to the seeds of low expectations there is protection from the threat of failure, but self-doubt is also thus transformed into a self-made prison. And it is a great tragedy to dwell for a lifetime in a prison of your own making, all the while possessing—but never using—the key that guarantees your release.

Almost everyone arrives in adulthood with their "gourds" filled with the seeds of self-doubt and both fists wrapped tightly around them. Life has a way of cramming the human brain with them, and then we squander decades watching them germinate into weeds of failure, passivity, and regret. But merely having the doubts does not lead to disappointment; clinging to them rather than escaping to freedom is the real culprit. Here are some notable examples of people who had every reason to doubt themselves, but chose instead the route of self-confidence.

Napoleon Bonaparte had the dubious distinction of finishing forty-second out of a graduating class of forty-three in military school. Nevertheless, he grew into a military genius, conquered most of Europe, rescued France from the anarchy that followed the French Revolution, discovered the Rosetta Stone, and established the Napoleonic Code of laws still used as a model by other countries.

Thomas Edison was repeatedly told by his own father that he was "stupid." Yet he became America's greatest inventor, creating the electric light bulb, the phonograph, wax paper, the printing telegraph, a magnetic ore separator, the electric trolley and a host of other devices. He owned 1,093 patents at his death.

Albert Einstein was nicknamed the *dummkopf* by his early elementary school teachers. His mother thought he was deformed due to the large size of his head. He barely spoke until the age of nine, but became the greatest theoretical physicist of all time.

Louis Pasteur was described by a school teacher as "the meekest, mildest, least-promising student in my class." He developed into France's greatest scientist. He was a groundbreaking chemist, the founder of physio-chemistry, the father of bacteriology, and the inventor of biotherapeutics.

Rod Serling wrote and marketed 40 TV scripts and short stories before he sold even one. Eventually, he won at least six Emmys for his writing, and had two successful television series, *The Twilight Zone* and *Night Gallery*.

One of **Sir Walter Scott's** teachers referred to his young student as a "blockhead" and said this of the future writer: "Dunce he was and dunce he will remain." His novels and poetry are still read today, and many of his works remain classics of English literature: *Ivanhoe, Rob Roy, The Lady of the Lake, Waverley, The Heart of Midlothian* and *The Bride of Lammermoor.*

The great explorer and aviation pioneer, **Admiral Richard Byrd** crash landed in his first two attempts to solo an airplane. He is now recognized as one of the greatest aviators of all time.

Walt Disney was fired from his job at the Kansas City Star newspaper, being told he had "lacked creativity." His first cartoon character, Oswald the Lucky Rabbit, was stolen by Universal Studios when they hired his entire staff from under him. His idea for Mickey Mouse was rejected for fear it would scare women. He is now, of course, recognized as a creative genius.

The first pass ever thrown in an NFL game by **Johnny Unitas** was intercepted and returned for a touchdown. The next time he touched the ball he fumbled it, and it was recovered by the opposition in the end zone for a touchdown. He is now believed by many to be the greatest quarterback ever to play the game of football.

"Colonel" Harland Sanders was a colossal failure throughout his life. He attempted careers as a soldier, a farm hand, a streetcar conductor, blacksmith's helper, rail-yard fireman, insurance salesman, tire salesman and service station operator, never achieving success. He even failed at marriage. When he retired, he used his first social security check to open a restaurant he called, "Kentucky Fried Chicken."

César Ritz was fired from his first hotel job by a boss who told him he had "no flair for the hospitality industry." He founded the Ritz-Carlton hotel chain.

Clint Eastwood was fired in 1959 by Universal Studios because his Adam's apple was too big. However, for the next 50 years he produced and acted in some of Hollywood's best and most popular films. He was nominated for six Oscars®, winning three, and has won dozens of other awards for his performances.

Burt Reynolds was fired by Universal Studios the very same day because he had "no talent as an actor." They were right! But he believed in himself anyway and became the most popular male actor of the seventies and early eighties.

In 1944, a teenage girl named Norma Jean Baker showed up at the Blue Book Modeling Agency in Manhattan seeking a job as a model. She was told by Mrs. Emmeline Snively, director of the agency, "Honey, you'd better learn secretarial work or else get married." Norma Jean then changed her name to **Marilyn Monroe** and became an enduring sex symbol and beauty icon. In 1946 alone, she appeared on the cover of 33 magazines.

Decca Records executive Paul Cohen called **Buddy Holly** "he biggest no-talent kid I've ever worked with." A year later, Holly's song, "That'll Be the Day," hit number one on the charts, followed by "Peggy Sue" and "Oh Boy!" Had he not been killed in a plane crash a year later at the age of 22, there would almost certainly have been many more.

The Decca Recording Company confirmed its lack of talent for spotting talent by rejecting **The Beatles** in 1962 with these words: "We don't like their sound. Guitar groups are on the way out." As it turned out, not only were such groups not on the way out, but the foursome became the most famous and popular rock and roll group of the 60s, and perhaps of all time.

In 1954, at the age of 19, **Elvis Presley** was fired from the cast of *The Grand Ole Opry* after just one performance. The manager of the famed country music venue, Mr. Jimmy Denny, told him, "Son, you'd better learn to drive a truck, 'cause you ain't goin' nowhere in the music business." A year later, Presley signed his first recording contract with RCA Records. To date, more than a billion of his records and CDs have sold worldwide, and more than 150 of his albums and singles have been certified gold, platinum, or multi-platinum, with others still to follow as sales continue more than three decades after his death.

Emmitt Smith, a star running back for Escambia High School in Pensacola, Florida, was recruited by the University of Florida. Recruiting guru Max Emfinger said of the high school senior, "Emmitt Smith is a lugger, not a runner. He's not fast. He can't get around the corner. When he falls flat on his face, remember where you heard it first." Smith was a consensus first-team All-America at Florida, and went on to become the all-time leading career rusher in the National Football League.

In the 1920s, **Lucille Ball** was a shy, awkward teenager who dreamed of making people laugh. She was elated at the age of 15 when her mother finally agreed to send her to the John Murray Anderson School for the Performing Arts in Manhattan. After only six weeks, her exasperated instructors told her mother to stop wasting her money by sending her back for a second term. They wrote, "Lucy's wasting her time and ours. She's too shy and reticent to put her best foot forward." Rubbing salt into the wound, none other than Mr. John Murray Anderson, himself, told the aspiring actress to "Try any other profession. Repeat… *any* other profession." She tried out for roles on Broadway but was told by a production assistant, "Go home. You weren't meant for show business." She landed one small role in a show chorus, but was fired before the first performance. She finally achieved success at the age of 40 with the hit television show, *I Love Lucy*. Half a century later, that show is still viewed by millions daily, and has never been off the air since it debuted in 1951. Lucille Ball remains one of the most beloved comedic actresses of the past century.

Wilma Rudolph did the seemingly impossible in 1960. She had been born prematurely and spent most of her early childhood in bed. The 20th of 22 children, there was never enough money to go around, and certainly not enough to properly care for her many ailments. She contracted mumps, measles, chicken pox, rubella, scarlet fever, and polio—all by the age of six. The polio deformed her left leg and turned her left foot severely inward. Twice each day, as the doctor had told her to do, Wilma's mother would strain to pull that left foot straight, often leaving little Wilma in tears. Doctors put the misshapen leg in a brace and told her she would never walk without it. But at the age of nine, she confounded them all when she ripped off the leg brace and took a few clumsy, faltering steps without it. By age 10 she was walking normally. A year later, her brothers put up a basketball hoop in the yard, and she played constantly. She joined her school team and set a state record one evening by scoring 49 points, and was awarded all-state honors. The school formed a track team specifically to take advantage of Wilma's speed and train her to do even better. She won a Bronze Medal in 1956 in the Melbourne, Australia Olympics. Four years later, in Rome, she became the first woman ever to win three gold medals in a single Olympic Games. The Italian media dubbed her "The Black Gazelle" and she was heralded as the fastest woman who had ever lived.

Phyllis Diller was a reporter for a small-town California newspaper, augmenting her income as a housemaid until the age of 37. At that time, in 1955, she was selected as a contestant on a television quiz show, *You Bet Your Life*, starring comedian Groucho Marx. The game itself was secondary to the ad-libbed interplay between Marx and the two contestants; Diller's witty comebacks and memorable laugh landed her a spot on the stage of San Francisco's legendary comedy club, The Purple Onion. She was a smash hit, playing for a record 87 straight weeks, and a new career was born in television, movies, comedy clubs and even Broadway. In 1992, the woman who scrubbed floors until almost the age of forty received the American Comedy Award for Lifetime Achievement.

Setbacks, criticisms, and mistakes like these are likely to burden anyone with an entire skull loaded with the seeds of self-doubt and the all-too-human tendency to cling tenaciously to the convenient excuses they provide. By the time we reach adulthood, each of us is laden with bushel baskets full of such doubts. But along with maturity also comes a gift that is indescribably wonderful: *the option to let go of them*. All of the men and women listed above garnered their share (and in some cases, *more* than their share) of seeds. Yet, somewhere in the jungle of life they each mustered the courage to release them, leave them behind and profoundly believe in themselves. Freedom comes when one dares to let go and experience the exhilarating liberty of high self-expectations, the unfettered delight of dreaming big dreams and fully anticipating their realization.

Chapter XII

AN ATTITUDE
OF PURPOSE

Happiness is rarely the product of a targeted search. More often, it sneaks up on us as we focus our resources on the fulfillment of a noble and generous cause. Perhaps the first step in finding joy comes in realizing that happiness is an intensely individual experience, not a relative one. In other words, enjoying happiness would be a lot easier if we didn't compare ourselves to others so much. In fact, I suspect that an essential ingredient of happiness in the reckoning of most people—even if only subconsciously—is not merely feeling happy, but feeling that I am *happier than others*. In other words, I reason that my feelings of happiness don't really count unless I'm actually happier than I think most other people are. If I suspect that other people—especially my friends, neighbors and coworkers—are happier than I am, the unfavorable comparison, itself, then makes me unhappy. More accurately, it *redefines* my happiness as unhappiness and I then feel compelled to set the bar for my own contentment at a higher level. I conclude that my feelings of happiness must be a "false positive" reading, like a test that might tell a woman she's pregnant when she's not. So I reject my upbeat mood in favor of what I have now deduced to be reality: "I must not *actually* be happy; my mind must be playing tricks on me." *Voilà!* My lightness of being has magically transformed itself into discontentment—though no outward change in circumstances has occurred. Because the very human tendency is to overestimate the happiness of others (after all, how many of the people we encounter in a day tell us *all* their troubles?), I have now set myself up for a miserable existence, one that demands that I pursue and reach an unattainable standard before I will allow myself to enjoy the satisfaction, peace of mind, and contentment I crave.

One of the most revealing findings of happiness research has been dubbed "The Easterlin Paradox." It notes three apparently inconsistent revelations. First, in any given society, rich people are happier than poor people. That stands to reason; the rich have fewer worries, more opportunities, nicer and more frequent vacations, better healthcare, etc. Secondly, though, rich countries are no happier than poor countries. Finally, and strangely, as societies grow richer they do not grow happier. The last two conclusions seem to contradict the first finding. On closer examination, however, they reinforce the relative nature of happiness: people view themselves as happy not in relation to how much progress they have made or how pleasant their circumstances may be, but in comparison to whether they are better off than their peers. Supporting this finding, a separate study reveals that the vast majority of Americans and Europeans have more material wealth and possessions than their parents did. However, the percentage of the population that is happy has *not* increased, and depression and anxiety rates have expanded dramatically. Other findings include these two interesting tidbits:

1) When an individual's income rises, but does so at a slower rate than that of the person's peers, happiness *decreases* despite the increase in wealth, and

2) When income rises, but more slowly than one had expected, happiness also decreases.

If we continue to cling to this relative method of assessing our own degree of contentment, we make it certain that no more than half of us —and probably far less than that— will ever know real satisfaction. Perhaps there is a better approach.

Constantly measuring my own happiness against the perceived happiness of others is a recipe for misery. In fact, seeing happiness as an end-in-itself will almost always bring me the exact opposite. Happiness is not a product; it is a by-product. Continual introspection and soul-searching in hopes of finding vestiges of happiness within the black recesses of my psyche puts my focus in precisely the wrong place: on me. True contentment—and often success, as well—comes as the result of focusing on other people and nobler causes. It is a paradox, but one whose timeless truthfulness resonates within us all. I can only become happy when I focus on bringing happiness to others. I can only fully enjoy life when I seek to help others fully enjoy theirs. I can only truly enjoy what I have, when I seek to make sure others have what they want or need. I achieve success as a result of helping those around me to succeed. Zig Ziglar told audiences for decades, "You can get everything you want in life if you will just help enough other people get what they want." Similarly, Mahatma Gandhi once wrote, "The best way to find yourself is to lose yourself in the service of others." Most succinctly of all, Winston Churchill wrote, "We make a living by what we get, but we make a life by what we give."

Philosophers and theologians through the centuries have theorized that those who seek happiness for themselves rarely find it, but those who strive to promote the happiness of others become happy as an indirect result of their own generosity. In turn, when the beneficiaries of such kindnesses express genuine gratitude for their windfall they, too, become happier. You've heard of a "vicious cycle." Call this the "Delicious Cycle" or the "Auspicious Cycle" or even the "Propitious Cycle." Whatever name you choose, it is one of the most wonderful laws of life: when you serve or give you make yourself *and* the beneficiary happier. "Cast your bread on the waters," Solomon wrote in the Old Testament book of Ecclesiastes, "and after many days it will return to you." When we find a noble cause, a "magnificent obsession," a mission we deem to be of greater importance than ourselves, that is when we experience true contentment. Ironically, until we find a cause that we would be willing to die for, we flounder helplessly trying to find something to truly live for.

Giving of your time and resources will almost invariably improve the quality of your life, but there are limits. For example, there are those dedicated individuals who are overwhelmed by the demands of caring for an incapacitated loved one. Such people may enjoy the knowledge that they are doing the right thing and honoring their commitments. They may deservedly congratulate themselves for their sense of duty, honor, and responsibility. They will likely be hailed by others as shining examples of selflessness. But they will rarely be happy, because the "giving" feels like an obligation, a task that has been foisted upon them rather than taken on as a voluntary act of love. A person who lives in, for example, Denmark and pays over 60% of his modest income in taxes each year may pat himself on the back for obeying the law and doing his civic duty. He may even feel comfortable that his tax dollars are providing needed government services, but merely surrendering to compulsory taxation does not result in the inner sense of satisfaction experienced by those who freely make a generous donation to charity. Capitulating to a demand does not produce the inner benefits that voluntary generosity does. Giving must be done freely, or it is not giving at all. Motive is critical. As the adage goes, "It's the thought that counts."

One of the most prominent researchers on the relationship between generosity and happiness is Canadian Dr. Elizabeth Dunn, professor of psychology at the University of British Columbia in Vancouver. For almost a decade, Dr. Dunn has investigated specifically how people respond emotionally to money spent on themselves versus money spent on others. Her findings show that people are much happier when they spend money on others, even if they don't realize it. Says Dunn, "We did a little experiment where we gave people some money, ten dollars, and we said, 'Hey, you can keep all this money for yourself or you can give as much of it as you want away.' What we found, consistent with all our past research, was that the more money people gave away the happier they felt. Conversely though, the more money people kept for themselves the more shame they experienced." Her team observed similar results at a business in Boston in which 16 workers were due to receive profit-sharing bonuses ranging from $3,000 to $8,000. Consistent with earlier studies, those who gave away a significant portion of their windfall experienced greater satisfaction than those who spent the money on themselves or saved it. In an unrelated 2003 study conducted at the University of Massachusetts Medical School, results showed that helping other people was more highly correlated with the giver's mental health than his or her religious activities, age, gender, stress level, income, or health. Another study revealed that there is strong correlation between the happiness, health and longevity of people who are emotionally and behaviorally compassionate.

Some people give because they believe the very act of giving will actually benefit them. Egocentric giving is a gift made with a self-serving motive. For example, I might bestow an expensive birthday present on the boss' son in order to curry favor with the head honcho. Or I could make a public donation to my *alma mater* so that I will be admired by my fellow alumni. Or I may perhaps volunteer at the local food bank in order to pad my resumé and appear more generous to a potential employer or college review board. Disgraced celebrities typically engage in very highly publicized acts of "goodwill" in order to rehabilitate their tarnished images. In such cases, a strict cost-to-benefits ratio has been calculated and the good-deed-doer has decided that parting with his time or money will bring him greater benefit than failing to do so. Their act of "generosity" is no nobler than buying a new car. When I engage in seemingly altruistic deeds, but from selfish motives, I have simply made a trade that I deem to be profitable to me. Selfish giving may bring a measure of fleeting satisfaction, just as getting a good deal on the new vehicle might, but giving for selfish reasons is not giving, at all. It is taking, loosely wrapped in a veneer of generosity. But only true generosity—that which is motivated by a genuine desire to help others—imparts lasting happiness on the giver.

Life is most fulfilling for those who live for a noble purpose. Their cause is not merely to make money or climb the corporate ladder or dwell in the biggest house. People who live primarily for material gain find their acquisitions surprisingly empty their satisfaction fleeting. They naturally conclude, therefore, that only amassing even more will bring them happiness. Perhaps their goal was too low, they reason. If a one-hundred-thousand dollar income didn't make them happy then perhaps two hundred thousand would, then half a million. If being promoted to supervisor didn't bring them lasting joy, perhaps manager will, then vice president. If the thrill of the 52-inch television wore off quickly, maybe the 60-inch would produce never-ending bliss. If constructing the new pool didn't fill their cup to overflowing, then maybe building a new home in a gated community with an even bigger pool and a hot tub would do the trick. Each time they raise the threshold and reach it they repeat the process. Eventually, they either collapse into a hopeless depression or anesthetize themselves with enough alcohol, drugs, or toys to distract them from their dilemma and prevent them from thinking too deeply about the void within. The wise man or woman learns early that money can buy a little happiness for a short while, but it purchases much more when it is given away.

Some people give for slightly less ignoble reasons. They contribute to charity in order to assuage their own guilt or to make themselves feel better. They enjoy the "warm glow" they feel inside when they give, and they seek to recreate it whenever they have spare change or extra time. For others, the primary motive behind their generosity is to earn a spot in heaven, or to fill their otherwise empty schedule by volunteering their time. Some do good in the belief that the recipients will then become obligated to return the favor when the need arises, or because they think fate will somehow keep score and bring them the same measure of good that they have done. Or maybe they donate to the poor because they reason that a generous society is less likely to become overrun with crime. They view their contribution as an investment in humanity which will help build a better future for themselves and their children and their children's children. All of these are acceptable motivations, but still fall short of the ideal. The happiest people believe that they bear a responsibility to give of their time and resources to those in need or to a noble cause. They do so not for their own personal gain, but because they believe they are doing the right thing. They dream of making a difference, of improving the lives of others, of leaving a lasting legacy of goodness. In short, they have a sense of purpose for their lives, and that purpose is a noble one.

THE IMPORTANCE OF PURPOSE

An individual who lacks purpose will experience little lasting happiness. Lacking a cause upon which to center your focus results in a sense of meaninglessness and fosters depression and passivity. Rather than summon your resources like a runner racing over a marked track toward a clearly defined finish line, the purposeless life degenerates into aimless wandering and an endless search for something to fill (or kill) time. On the surface, this may seem to be a pleasant existence. Rather than being driven to rise early, work feverishly and have little free time, people without a purpose can enjoy lots of leisure. In practice, however, the opposite is true. People who exhibit a strong sense of purpose enjoy their work more than those who lack it enjoy their leisure. Furthermore, those driven to strive mightily toward the fulfillment of their mission also relish and savor their scant free time all the more. Sándor Ferenczi, a psychoanalyst in the early 1900's, discovered that anxiety and depression occurred more often on Sundays than any other day of the week. Since that time, many observers have noted that vacations and retirement also tend to produce anxiety and depression. Work is stressful but, apparently, *not* working is even more so. It is, ironically, quite difficult to enjoy recreation unless there is plenty of work to do afterwards. A clear purpose focuses the mind. An unfocused mind wanders, and it generally wanders into negativity and obsesses over unresolved problems and anxiety-producing issues. Your occupation may temporarily fill the void of a true purpose for your life, but it is no substitute for having a higher calling than merely earning a paycheck. If you do not know *your* life purpose, your job can at least give you a short-term goal. But the type of purpose that fulfills goes beyond just working at a given task in order to pay the bills. Ultimate purpose comes from within and drives you toward an important objective, hopefully throughout your life.

History is replete with examples of highly successful people who retired from their lifelong profession or mission and died shortly thereafter. Alexander the Great conquered the world by the age of 33, wept "that there were no more worlds to conquer," and died. Charles Shultz, creator of the *Peanuts* comic strip which ran for half a century announced in December of 1999 that his final cartoon would appear on February 13, 2000. He died in his sleep the night before it ran. Andy Rooney, who delivered a commentary on CBS' long-running news program *60 Minutes*, retired from that position after more than thirty years, and died a month later. Any purpose—even a self-serving one—is better than none, but a noble purpose is the most fulfilling of all. Many other examples could be cited to support the idea that a sense of purpose correlates strongly with happiness. At different stages of life, the specific nature of your life's purpose may change—the only necessary constant is the nobility of the cause.

Many older individuals, in particular, find a new purpose for themselves after retirement. In earlier years, their cause may have been related to their children or to their jobs. But once their nest is empty and the career is in the rearview mirror, a shift naturally takes place. In later years, many seniors find renewed meaning by volunteering for charitable causes, and a growing body of sociological research has demonstrated that those who do volunteer gain as much as the intended beneficiaries. A number of studies have shown that older adults who volunteer regularly tend to be happier as a group than those who don't volunteer. According to Neenah L. Chappel in a 1999 research project, "Studies demonstrate that 70% of older volunteers claim to enjoy a better quality of life than the average non-volunteer." A 1999 survey by the Seniors Research Group, showed that 52% of senior citizens who volunteer frequently say that they are very satisfied with life, compared with 45% of occasional volunteers and only 37% of those who never volunteer. In addition, the benefits of volunteering appear to grow over time. Marc A. Musick and John Wilson reported in January 2003 that among the participants in a long-term study, people who were involved in volunteering at the beginning of the study were, as a group, less likely to be depressed eight years later. According to the most recent research, altruism increases your happiness by 27%. Stated another way, when you choose to be selfish, you are thereby reducing your happiness by 27%. Your mission in life may also change due to your circumstances, regardless of your age.

Regardless of your situation, adopting a specific purpose for your existence and possessing a clear reason to live tends to extend and improve the quality of your life. Viktor Frankl, the Jewish psychiatrist who endured years in Theresienstadt Concentration Camp in modern-day Czech Republic, wrote the following words in his classic book, *Man's Search for Meaning*:

The meaning of life differs from person to person, from day to day and from hour to hour. What matters, therefore, is not the meaning of life in general but rather the specific meaning of a person's life at a given moment. To put the question in general terms would be comparable to the question posed to a chess champion, "Tell me, Master, what is the best move in the world?" There simply is no such thing as the best or even a good move apart from a particular situation in a game and the particular personality of one's opponent. The same holds true for human existence. One should not search for an abstract meaning of life. Everyone has his own specific vocation or mission in life to carry out a concrete assignment which demands fulfillment.

Despite the profundity of Frankl's insight, I suspect that he possessed a lifelong mission—to help people live more fulfilling lives—that manifested itself in various ways and in a wide variety of situations. While the *method* of carrying out that mission changed from day to day and place to place, his overarching purpose (as evidenced in his chosen profession) remained fundamentally unchanged. Though a chess master's best possible move changes each time the position of the pieces on the board is altered, his ultimate goal of winning—his purpose, if you will—stays constant.

During World War II, Frankl was stripped of his every possession prior to his imprisonment by the Nazis. Far worse, he lost his wife, his brother and both parents in that ghastly place. Even amid such horrors, he managed to find meaning by striving to encourage his fellow prisoners not to give up hope. Even when confronted by unspeakable atrocities, he consciously sought to fulfill his purpose in life. Later, he would write, "What man actually needs is not a tension-less state but rather the striving and struggling for some goal worthy of him. What he needs is not the discharge of tension at any cost, but the call of a potential meaning waiting to be fulfilled by him." While imprisoned, the manifestation of Frankl's purpose was to prevent his fellow prisoners from committing suicide. There was a strict policy against intervening in an attempted suicide in those camps and anyone caught trying to rescue a person who had just hung himself, for example, would be punished severely. So Frankl sought to prevent the attempt, itself. On two occasions, prisoners confided in Frankl that they had resolved to kill themselves because they had nothing left to expect from life. The future seemed to hold nothing other than suffering, torture, and death. Frankl sought to convince them that though they expected nothing of life, life still expected something *from them*. One was a scientist whose voluminous works were, as yet, still incomplete. Only he would be capable of finishing the work. The other was reminded that he had a child who was safe in another country and needed his father. Frankl's purpose never changed, whether as a prewar psychiatrist, an imprisoned encourager, or a postwar author.

DISCOVERING YOUR PURPOSE

Some people have an innate sense of purpose that they have never doubted; most of us, however, meander through life wondering what our purpose might be. There are very few Mother Teresas, Billy Grahams, Mohandas Gandhis or Martin Luther Kings in the world, those who discover their reason for living early in life and pursue it with passion until their deaths. Each of those four examples was driven by religious conviction, but many quite irreligious people have enjoyed similar passion and focus. Albert Einstein was an atheist, but his headlong determination to solve the mysteries of the universe drove him until the age of 70. At that point, having reached all of his goals, he assumed that he had expended all of his useful energies and retired. He became listless, bored, and depressed. Then, he suddenly realized that he could create a new purpose for his life: to develop a plan to control the destructive potential of nuclear power and to find peaceful uses for it. Suddenly, his fervor was rekindled. His new sense of purpose drove him until his death half a dozen years later. But Einstein was the exception; for most of us life's purpose is not created, it is discovered. More accurately, it is uncovered. It is already within us and merely needs to be detected.

Locked up within each of us lies a noble dream, a sense that we have something of importance to contribute to the world and a longing to do it, a life purpose that seeks expression. Though it may have been beaten down by struggles or shoved aside in favor of more pressing matters, it still lurks there and needs merely to be rediscovered and unleashed. The mere fact that it already exists, and therefore need not be manufactured, should come as an encouragement to those aimless souls who meander through life's maze in hopes of stumbling across their *raison d'être*. The task of finding one's reason for living is thus transformed from the quite daunting undertaking of inventing and building a prototype from scratch into the more manageable one of merely finding it in a cluttered closet. Unearthing it is vital because, as we have established, people who do good also do well. There is an unmistakable link between those who strive to make the world a better place and those who enjoy their lives in this world most. The formula for finding your purpose is a simple one.

First, imagine yourself on your deathbed, hopefully many years in the future. As you envision yourself looking back on five to seven decades of toil, striving and effort, which memories will bring you the most satisfaction, the feeling of having enjoyed a life well-lived? What do you fear you will regret most? What will you be proudest of? Will there be a sense of wasted time and squandered opportunities? As you recall your many life goals and dreams, which ones will occupy most of your thoughts? Now, rank those goals in terms of which will seem most important to you at that time. You might even graph your life in terms of the times when life will have been the most fulfilling or the least satisfying. What do those times have in common with one another? Now, picture yourself a few days later at your own funeral. What do you hope your spouse, your friends, your children, and your relatives will say about you? What do you hope they will list as your greatest accomplishments? What words would you like engraved on your tomb stone? Most importantly, are you doing those things *now*?

To find your purpose in life, you next need to examine your deepest longings in the present. Ask yourself a few more questions:

1) Which activities bring me the most personal satisfaction?

2) What makes me feel good about myself? What bestows on me the warmest of the warm glows described earlier in this chapter?

3) What activities bring me the biggest smiles?

4) What do I enjoy most?

5) Is there a person (or a few people) whose biographies so inspire me that I wish I could live their lives and enjoy their accomplishments?

6) Are there any activities that cause me to lose track of time?

7) If I had unlimited resources, what would I spend my time doing?

8) If I was forced by law to leave all my belongings to one—and only one—charity, to which cause would I donate them? Why?

The way you answer these questions provides strong clues regarding your unique purpose in life. Aligning your current activities with the priorities revealed by this exercise will then become a very important step in fulfilling that purpose.

With the above questions answered, a strong pattern is likely to emerge. One, two or three powerful, life-focusing priorities will probably evidence themselves, and these will represent your purpose in life, your mission and your key to happiness. Once these have been established, you must now take the bold step of building your life around them. Is your career aligned with your purpose? If not, is there a way to integrate the two? Should you or could you change careers, or make plans to do so in the future? If the two cannot be aligned, or if changing careers isn't feasible, perhaps your job will become merely a way to pay your bills as you focus on your purpose while off the clock. But the most critical step is to make a conscious decision to center your life, your energies, your budget, and your time around your purpose. Only in so doing do you create the potential for a life that is filled with meaning.

Chapter XIII

An Attitude
of Persistence

Nothing in the world can take the places of persistence. Talent will not; nothing is more common than unsuccessful men with talent. Genius will not; unrewarded genius is almost a proverb. Education will not; the world is full of educated failures. Persistence and determination alone are omnipotent. The slogan "press on" has solved and always will solve the problems of the human race.

Calvin Coolidge

All of the attitudes written of in this book will not amount to much unless you possess the quality of persistence, the ability and willingness to stick with a project no matter what obstacles might stand in your way. Perseverance transcends mere motivation. Motivation drives you to pursue your goals; persistence refuses to allow you to give up or even slow down when that motivation ebbs and the goals appear unattainable. Perseverance is the bulldog tenacity that forces a weightlifter to continue pumping iron during those months when no progress is apparent. Perseverance is the determination to keep typing even when it seems no one will ever read what you're writing. It is the resolve to keep marketing even when sales are few and far between. Persistence is the strength of mind required to push through mental barriers and continue slogging, punching, pushing, driving for the objective. It expresses that subtle intangible something in the brain that refuses to define a task as "banging your head against a wall" or "beating a dead horse" and instead describes it as one of those myriad of "if-at-first-you-don't-succeed cases." It is essential.

Persistence doesn't mean repeating a fruitless task *ad infinitum*. It might mean pursuing the same worthy goal, but by a different means. The greatest of American inventors, Thomas Edison, was interviewed by a young reporter who had the temerity to ask Mr. Edison if he felt like a failure over his thousands of unsuccessful attempts to create an electric light. Edison is alleged to have replied, "Young man, why would I feel like a failure? And why would I ever give up? I now know definitively over 9,000 ways that an electric light bulb will not work. Success is almost in my grasp." And shortly after that, after exceeding 10,000 attempts, Edison invented the light bulb. And the substance he finally found that would produce a lasting filament? *Bamboo.* Yes, bamboo. His willingness to try any and every substance on earth—no matter how far-fetched its potential for success might seem—resulted in his ultimate success.

Persistence is not testing the same substance ten thousand times; that is idiocy. Persistence is relentlessly searching for new substances to test, with the ultimate goal having never changed. Edison is quoted as saying, "Many of life's failures are people who did not realize how close they were to success when they gave up." What if he had given up after only 9,500 attempts? The Wizard of Menlo Park, as he came to be known, summed up his philosophy of life in this 1903 statement: "Genius is one percent inspiration, ninety-nine percent perspiration. None of my inventions came by accident. I see a worthwhile need to be met and I make trial after trial until it comes."

Milton Hershey dropped out of school in the fourth grade, and became an apprentice to a printer. He was fired. He then became an apprentice to a candy-maker in Lancaster, Pennsylvania and spent four years learning the business. However, his first three candy companies were failures. His fourth, the Lancaster Caramel Company, was a big success. Unsatisfied, however, he sold the business and began the Hershey Company, a name which is now synonymous with milk chocolate.

Simon Cowell, now famous for his series, *American Idol* and *The X Factor*, was also a dropout, having left school at the age of 15. He took a job in the mail room at EMI Music, then was promoted to the A&R section (Artists and Repertoire, the division that finds new musical talent and serves as liaison between the artist and the recording label). He then founded E & S Music, a company that went belly-up in its first year. Then he took a job with Fanfare Records and was an instant success. Later, on his own, he built the music empire that has made him fabulously wealthy and successful.

Johnny Unitas, cited earlier in this book as an example of self-confidence, was also a paragon of persistence. As a high school senior, he wanted to play football at the University of Notre Dame, but the coaches told him he was too small (145 pounds) to play college football. He was offered a scholarship at the University of Pittsburgh, but failed the entrance exam. He finally succeeded at playing quarterback for the University of Louisville, but after graduation he was not drafted until the ninth round, and was ultimately cut by the Pittsburgh Steelers. He called the Cleveland Browns for a tryout, but was told they were not looking for a quarterback. He then played semi-pro football in Pittsburgh for six dollars per game. He hung a tire in the park and practiced throwing the football through it, sometimes while running full speed, to increase his accuracy. The following year, he was granted a tryout with the Baltimore Colts, and his career is now the stuff of legend.

J.K. Rowling, the author of the immensely popular *Harry Potter* series, wasn't always a success. While writing her first book she endured a divorce and moved into a tiny apartment with her infant daughter, Jessica. Clinically depressed and, at times, suicidal she was driven to write about pain, loss, and death. Unable to support herself, she survived on welfare. She was unable to find work and regarded herself as "the biggest failure I knew." She used her free time to write the first book in what would become the best-selling series of all time: *Harry Potter and the Sorcerer's Stone*. It was rejected by 12 publishers. Even Barry Cunningham, the Bloomsbury Publishing Company editor who finally agreed to publish the book advised Rowling to "get a day job," telling her there was little chance she'd ever make any money selling children's books. The seven *Harry Potter* fantasies have now been made into eight motion pictures and translated into 67 languages. Her last four novels in the series hold the top four spots as the fastest-selling books in history, and she is now rumored to be worth 15 billion dollars.

One of the most inspiring examples of persistence comes from Hollywood in the *Rocky* movies. This popular film series spanned six films over 30 years (1976-2006) and features a boxer who makes up for his lack of brains, size, and talent with raw guts and tenacity. Beaten bloody in almost every fight, knocked down repeatedly, he refuses to stay on the mat. He is the embodiment of the phrase "down, but not out." In the final film, Rocky Balboa is 59 years old and decides to come out of retirement one last time. His son, Rocky Jr., is now a grown man and has opted to don a business suit, live the life of a corporate employee and call himself "Robert." He blames his lack of success on living in his father's celebrity shadow, and begs him not to return to the ring. In the most poignant scene in the film, Rocky confronts his son on a deserted street and delivers the following speech:

"Let me tell you something you already know. The world ain't all sunshine and rainbows. It's a very mean and nasty place and it will beat you to your knees and keep you there permanently if you let it. You, me, or nobody is gonna hit as hard as life. But it ain't about how hard you hit; it's about how hard you can get hit, and keep moving forward, how much you can take, and keep moving forward. That's how winning is done. Now, if you know what you're worth, then go out and get what you're worth. But you gotta be willing to take the hits, and not pointing fingers saying you ain't where you wanna be because

*of him, or her, or anybody. Cowards do that and that
ain't you. You're better than that!"*

The *Rocky* series can be summed up in one of those sen-
tences: "It's not how hard you can hit, it's how hard you can
get hit and keep moving forward, how much you can take
and keep moving forward." It also helps sum up the life of a
highly successful person.

Perseverance proves elusive due to a faulty line of reasoning that seems, on the surface, to be sound. Patterns
that unfold repeatedly in life naturally spawn the belief that
the mold is unbreakable, the habit intractable, the routine
permanent. For example, if I have tried repeatedly to lose
twenty pounds, but invariably pack back on any weight I've
lost, I will eventually surrender to the "undeniable fact" that
I can never permanently lose weight. With this supposed fact
in hand, I have effectively undercut any reason to persevere.
After all, if I already know that my efforts are doomed to
fail, why endure the pain that comes with denying myself
day after day. A simple syllogism sums up the argument:

A: I hate dieting. I always have; I always will.

B: My hatred of dieting inevitably leads to gaining
back any weight I've lost.

C: If I already know I'm going to give up on my diet
eventually, why not go ahead and surrender from
the very start so I don't have to endure the pain of
dieting at all?

The flaw in the argument is in the presupposition, "A."
The little known fact (little known because so few persevere
long enough to discover it) is that if one persists in a hated
behavior long enough, eventually he or she will stop hating

it, embrace it and even enjoy that behavior. This is the Law of Cognitive Dissonance.

Cognitive Dissonance is the term chosen by psychologists to describe the inner anxiety created when a person's behavior does not match his belief system. A woman who greatly values tranquility, but works in a hectic, frenzied workplace will not merely feel uncomfortable; she will feel, "I don't belong here. This isn't who I am." When exposed to this cacophony and mayhem for an extended time, the sentiment will morph into a desperate feeling of, "Something's gotta give." The man who loves his wife and genuinely meant his vows, yet nevertheless strays into an affair with another woman, will sense almost unrelenting dissonance. A war of words transfixes his brain:

"I can't keep doing this."

"But I don't want to stop. This is exciting."

"Yeah, but it's wrong."

"How can it be wrong when it feels so wonderful? Maybe the rules are all wrong."

"I took a vow not to do this."

"Yeah, but she took a vow to love and cherish *me*, too. How long did *that* last?"

The inner conversation continues *ad nauseum*, but the feeling is unrelenting: "I have to stop this. This isn't right. It's not who I am."

Eventually, however, one of the two internal voices will begin to grow fainter and more distant until it is silenced altogether. This is the law of cognitive dissonance. Either the woman will quit her frenzied workplace and find elsewhere the tranquility she longs for or she will adapt and begin to flourish and thrive in her fast-paced environment. The adulterous man will either end his affair and return to the faithful marriage he believes in, or he will deem the belief system to be archaic or inapplicable and thus squelch the feelings of guilt so that he may continue the illicit relationship. But the process works in reverse as well.

The unavoidable reality of cognitive dissonance can be harnessed to work in your favor. That is, you can deliberately place yourself in a position that creates dissonance and then persevere in that behavior until the belief system crumbles. The behavior is then adopted by the subconscious mind as an acceptable and routine aspect of your new lifestyle. I once hated the very idea of weightlifting. I was skinny through my twenties, then began gaining weight and developing a potbelly in my early thirties. It was then that I decided to test the theory of cognitive dissonance and resolved to lift weights *until I started liking it*. The temptation to quit was strong, for inertia resisted my efforts to change and exerted a powerful pull toward my former habits. But I persisted. I went to the gym every other day and went through my complete exercise routine in 15 minutes flat, pumping the weights as rapidly as I possibly could, increasing the weight and repeating the set, then running to the next machine and doing as many sets and reps as my body would tolerate. I hated the practice so much that I feared that if I took more time for my exercise that I would begin to rationalize that I couldn't afford to spend so long in the gym and my work would suffer, tempting me to conclude that I "ought to" quit for the good of my career. The dissonance between my belief ("I hate pumping iron.") and my practice (continual trips to the weight room) was tremendous. But as months of dogged perseverance exacted their toll on my belief system, I slowly began to hate my regimen less. I began to enjoy my newfound strength and the appreciation my wife had for my toned physique. I loved it when the amount of weight I could bench press steadily climbed. After more than a year of persistence, I found that I no longer need to persevere at all. I *wanted* to go to the gym and lift weights. I loved it! I paid trainers to take me further in my efforts to strengthen and tone my body. Now, 20 years later, I still regularly go to the weight room. If I fail to do so, I experience... *cognitive dissonance!* The very force that once caused me to flee the gym now compels me to return again and again. Most people assume that fighting the current for a lifetime is an exhausting and futile task. They fail to realize that if you fight the current long enough, it will eventually relent and reverse its flow. From that day forward, you will enjoy the luxury of being carried by it in the direction you wish to go.

Moving beyond Negatudes to Megatudes lies at the core of changing the direction of your life. But this is not a process that will take place on its own. Nor is it one that occurs simply because you are merely able to name and describe life's twelve Megatudes. Each one is a quality that must be carefully monitored and acted upon until each becomes second nature to you. Like the front-end alignment on your car, priorities cannot be established at a moment in time and left alone from that point forward. Quite the contrary, they must be checked-on and tweaked regularly throughout the course of your life, for there is the constant tendency for values to drift, and always in the wrong direction. Like a room that predictably becomes more disorganized, dirty, dusty, and decrepit when not maintained, your existence will naturally deteriorate unless you exert conscious and active efforts to resist this backward trend. The day you stop building your future is the day you will begin to die. The day you cease infusing your soul with life's Megatudes is the day you will slowly begin sliding into Negatudes. Life has no neutral gear. You will always be moving forward or backward, and because the trail of life rises before you (and falls behind you), taking your foot off the accelerator will necessarily result in backsliding. You must choose between a downward roll or an upward climb. The former requires no effort at all, for it is the default path of life; even a dead fish can travel downstream. The latter requires relentless work over a period of decades, but the rewards of this labor are sweet, and they represent the life you were born to live.

TODAY

*T*oday *is a very important day, because what I do today will change my future. The choices I make today—even the small ones—will either make my life better or they will make it worse, so I will choose wisely. The decisions I make today will either advance my career or damage it; they will improve my relationships or harm them; they will increase my income or decrease it; they will improve my health or undermine it; they will enhance my reputation or soil it; they will strengthen my character or weaken it; they will either sweeten my well or they will contaminate it. Therefore, I will carefully consider how I spend my time today, what I say, how I say it, what I do, with whom I spend my time and what I put in my body. I will plan my day according to my priorities, rather than let it be planned for me by pressures or by the demands of others. I will guard my mind from negativity and pessimism, because whatever I allow to pollute my well will eventually pollute my life. I will flood my mind with positive thoughts and input. I will expect good things to happen. I will face each challenge with calmness, clarity, and a smile. Today is, indeed, a VERY important day.* *

ABOUT THE AUTHOR

Billy Riggs has been called "The Dr. Phil of Magic," and is America's source for all things attitude! Through books, recordings, and live keynote speeches Billy uses an unusual blend of comedy, music, magic, and motivation to spread his positive attitude to millions of people on five continents. A spellbinding communicator, Mr. Riggs honed his uplifting message and speaking skills in the pulpit, founding one of America's fastest-growing churches at the age of 29. Though his presentations now are secular, audiences sometimes sense the old preacher in him, stirred by his sincerity and power on the platform. In 2002, Mr. Riggs was presented the highest earned award of the National Speakers Association: the Certified Speaking Professional, or CSP. Since 1995, he has breathed **The Magic of Attitude** into people, companies, and organizations.

But the goose bumps aren't always the result of dramatic oratory! When Billy Riggs appears, things on stage begin to *disappear!* Using world-class magical illusions to drive his points home, Billy's presentations have transformed hundreds of otherwise ordinary conferences into something truly special. His quick wit and quicker hands spread laughter and raise morale as listeners learn to reshape their destinies by eliminating their "Grand Illusions" and embracing even grander truths.

Billy Riggs lives in Austin, Texas with his wife and son.

Billy Riggs Speaks at Conferences

Master *DIS*-illusionist!

If you enjoyed this book, you'll *love* hearing Billy in person! When his powerful message is combined with magic and comedy, the result is a keynote that is a rollercoaster of laughter, inspiration and learning. Businesses, associations, chambers of commerce, school districts, government agencies, and charities have all proclaimed his programs as the best they've ever experienced. With 30 years performing on 5 continents and 12 cruise ships, he has experience you can trust.

Available programs include:

Positively Magical Selling!	for salespeople
How to Achieve the Impossible!	for managers
The Power of a P.M.A.	for everyone
Positively Magical Service!	for service providers
The Magic of Network Marketing!	for MLMs
Beyond Belief!	for youth

As seen on PBS!

Billy Riggs, Master *DIS*-illusionist!
www.billyriggs.com

1) Character
2) Relationships
3) Achievement (toward a worthy goal)
4) Faith (in the widest sense – to
     get a higher purpose in your life)
5) Your personal attitude!